You Thought You Couldn't Change, Either

Andre' Gilchrist

Bloomington, IN   Milton Keynes, UK

AuthorHouse™
1663 Liberty Drive, Suite 200
Bloomington, IN 47403
www.authorhouse.com
Phone: 1-800-839-8640

AuthorHouse™ UK Ltd.
500 Avebury Boulevard
Central Milton Keynes, MK9 2BE
www.authorhouse.co.uk
Phone: 08001974150

© 2006 Andre' Gilchrist. All rights reserved.

No part of this book may be reproduced, stored in a retrieval system, or transmitted by any means without the written permission of the author.

First published by AuthorHouse 2/22/2006

ISBN: 1-4259-1310-5 (sc)

Printed in the United States of America
Bloomington, Indiana

This book is printed on acid-free paper.

ACKNOWLEDGMENTS

One of my favorite sayings is *"it takes a whole village to raise a child."* The person I am today is not the person I was many years ago. It is not due to the influence or example of one individual but that of many. I do not have the time or space here to mention everyone that has shaped me but there are certain individuals I need to thank because if not for their individual and collective influence and experience this work would not be possible.

First of all and most important I want to thank God because if not for his loving care and intervention in my life I wouldn't be here today. I also want to give thanks to God for whatever writing ability I have been blessed to possess is only through God's loving kindness, grace and mercy.

I want to give thanks to my deceased mother, father, and brother, (Effie Gilchrist, Hubert Gilchrist, & Hubert Gilchrist, Jr). Even though you are not with me in body I know that you are here in spirit. A day doesn't go by when you aren't in my thoughts. Even though the things I have accomplished in my life I did not achieve them in your lifetime, your teachings and the way you lived your life has been an inspiration to me and allowed me the courage to live my life the way it is today. The person that I have become today is a direct result of the upbringing I received from you. To my father as much as I was determined not to be like you today I strive to be just like you. To my mother your desire and willingness to help other people regardless of their age, race, sexual identity or religion is a prime motivator in my life today that allows me the drive to help those less fortune than myself. To my brother, watching the way you treated women has allowed me the ability to know today how I do not want to treat them.

I have only a few number of relatives left in this world. Because of that I have learned how to treasure you even more. To my aunts Mary William's and Bobby Askew, my cousin's Faye William's and Peggy Gilchrist, I am so grateful that God has allowed you to remain an active ingredient in my life. The ability to accept me as I am regardless of the things I have done in the past has given me the willingness to try and accept others on that same basis. To my cousins Najee and Jasime, seeing that there is no real male model in your life this new opportunity that God has given me to live a second life before I leave this world has given me the chance to be that male model in your life.

I want to thank certain people who helped and aided me through my educational journey. I want to thank President Cary Israel of Texas who during his short tenure at Raritan Valley Community College helped transfer that institution into a renowned institution of higher learning. At the same time taught me that there is nothing wrong with being a leader and inspiration to others. I will always remember your favorite saying, ***"never sweat the small stuff and remember everything is small stuff."*** I want to thank you for your leadership and guidance in my life. Not only was you my mentor and friend but also my role model and substitute father. You presented me with an image of an individual that inspired me to emulate and hope I affected other young people in the same fashion. Even though you are miles away and my only communication with you is through e-mails you continue to be a major influence in my life. It is a blessing knowing that whatever I might be going through and am need of some guidance and leadership all I need to do is send you an e-mail. You are such an integral part of my life that whatever I achieve I must humble myself and admit it is only through God's placement of you in my life. I want to thank Professor Carroll Wilson and Professor Tucker of the Raritan Valley Community College English department for help molding and shaping my love of writing into a form of communication that makes sense for everyone who reads it. I want to thank Professor Wilson for his training in editing manuscripts that would allow me to edit this manuscript myself. I want to thank Professor John Pace of the Essex Community College who taught me so much about life and people during my two year term as statewide President of the New Jersey Student College Coalition.

There are so many people that have influenced and had such a big impact in my life that I think it would be an injustice if I did not make an honest attempt at showing my appreciation to them. I need to thank Gwen, Nat, Mary, Trish, Mike, Renee, Alan, Mustafa, Steve (Mu-Fy), Diane, Curtis, Hugh, Al, Lorintha, Melvin C., Percell, Shakur, Nabiliah,

Claire, Chuck, Melinda, Cordell, Eve, Nate, Juanita, James, John, Mary Jo, Kareem, Lonnie, Marshall, Jerome, Rock, Vincent, Robert, Rex, Tracy, Will and Wajid. I want to give a special thanks to my good friend Abbe Brown, whom I have known since childhood and has always been an inspiration and motivator to me regardless of the things I might have done. These people and so many more individually and collectively have had such a monumential impact on my life I can't think of the words that would do justice to show my appreciation and gratitude.

    I want to thank my good friend, Mrs. Pazzetta Scott (who has relocated to Las Vegas) for being my friend no matter what I have went through. I want to thank her for being here for me today even though you live thousands of miles away. Mrs. Pazzetta Scott, even though you live in Las Vegas I enjoy the confort in knowing that if I need you that you are only a phone call away. I want to thank Mrs. Amanda Rivers for being my mother's best friend. I want to thank you for being there for me today after her death. Many people would have left after all the things I put you through but you stayed right there and helped me out. I have learned how to apply the principles of patience and tolerance in my life by watching how you have applied them in connection with your relationship with me.

    I want to thank my good friend Camose Thomissini for being my confidant and always raising my spirits when I was feeling down on myself. Many times when I have felt like what's the use you have always come up with the right things to say to give me the courage and energy to press on. I want to thank you for accepting me as the person I am today and not the person I was. Your acceptance of me gave me the strength and conviction of mind to allow people to see the real Andre for the first time. The strength and willingness it takes to honestly look at one's self comes from the motivation and support I have received from you. I want to thank you for convincing me that this is a project I should take on. I want to thank you for your faith and confidence in me, which has given me the courage to go on and attempt this piece of literary work. I have heard it said before that the type of person one is a direct reflection on the type of people that we associate with. Because of you Camose, I understand today truly what that statement means.

    I want to thank Deacon Henry Jones for your spiritual guidance once I decided that I wanted to come back to God and church. I want to thank the membership of Saint Paul Baptist Church for allowing me the opportunity to use the church property to give back to my community. I want to thank the church for allowing me the opportunity to help those indiviudals trying to find themselves trapped in the horrors of active addiction to find themselves back to reality.

I want to thank all of the legislators and politicians in New Jersey who serve on the local and state level for allowing me to see and witness the internal blessings one receives from being of service to their fellowman, without looking for anything in return. Today, I understand the philosophy of giving of oneself in order for that person to continue growing. It is only through the process of looking into oneself and seeing the kind of person I want to be and treated can I reciprocate and do the same towards my fellowman.

I want to thank all my friends all over the world that have had a lasting influence on me and loved me in spite of myself. Thank you and ***I LOVE YOU ALL.***

Lastly, I want to dedicate this book to people everywhere. My extreme desire is that anyone regardless of age, race, sex, creed, religion or lack of religion, who have found themselves caught up in the bowls of active addiction, to remember this. ***IF I CAN CHANGE SO CAN YOU___***

PREFACE

A few years ago I went to visit my cousin in Atlanta, Georgia. She had taken me to the final resting-place of the late Reverend Dr. Martin Luther King, Jr. Inside one of *the buildings adjacent to his final resting-place was this writing on the wall,* **"The richer we have become materially the poorer we have become morally and spiritually. We have learned to fly the air like birds and swim the sea like fish, but we have not learned the simple art of living together as brothers."** *This writing is one of the many writings of Dr. King that has stayed with me and has inspired me to write this manuscript. I identify with the above re*ading because I found out that the more I lived in a negative lifestyle the more I became involved in my own selfish desires. The more I became involved in narcotics the more I found myself moving further away from living morally and spiritually and not being able to live in this life with my fellow man.

This is the story of one individuals struggle within himself. Even though it seemed at times like he would lose the struggle he never gave up. This is the story of one individuals journey from desperation to determination. The story of one individual who found the answer to the question of why me to why not me. The story of one individuals story of exposing one's weaknesses to having those weaknesses manifest themselves later in that individual as strengths. This is the story of an individual who has come to understand what John Doe's statement meant, **"no man is an island entire of itself. Everyman is a piece of the continent a part of the mane. Whatever affects one; effects all because we are all involved in mankind. So never wonder for whom the bell tolls it tolls for thee."** This is the story of an individual who has learned what that statement means in today's world and how it applies to himself.

I am writing this in the hope that others might read it. In the hope that if they are going through the same thing or knows someone who is going through the same thing that they can pass on to them that here is an individual who thought he couldn't change and look at him now. I hope that people will see that here is an individual who is learning the art of living together with other people as brothers regardless of their age, race, color, creed, religion or lack or religion. Just like diversity is one of the strengths that makes this country great; this individual has learned that having diversity in his life is truly a blessing.

The second part of this book deals with the life and struggles of Andre Gilchrist and a more intense look into the internal structure of this individual. This section deals with **"Fear of Intimacy"** or as I like to refer to it as **"In To Me I See".** But as I am so often reminded that we are each other's eyes and ears.

Many days I ponder on the question on why is my life the way it is. I wonder why do people perceive me the way they do or more importantly how do I perceive myself. It takes a great amount of strength and courage to have the capacity to look inside oneself. Before I can be honest with anyone else it is imperative to my ongrowing growth in today's life and society that I be truly honest with myself.

To truly benefit from what this life has to offer me I need to be willing to take an internal look at myself and examine the reason behind the things I did and the motivation behind those actions. I have heard humility described as "not thinking less of one's self but thinking of one's self less." The only way to truly achieve humility is to look truly at one's self and have the strength and willingness to make the necessary changes.

So when we think of what intimacy means and how to apply it to our lives the first step is self-acceptance. I can not expect anyone to accept me if I haven't learned to accept myself first with all of my strengths and weaknesses. I have learned in this life's process that intimacy is so much more than a physical action between a man and a woman. It deals with allowing other people to see who we really are when all of the masks have been removed. It deals with the strength to allow others to see our vulnerabilities and not look at them as some sort of moral decay or weakness. It deals with the ability to allow our vulnerabilities to manifest themselves into our lives as God given assets. This process of becoming intimate with oneself is the beginning step to living a life full of serenity and happiness.

So I pray for God's will to grant me the strength and courage to take an honest and internal look at myself and become comfortable with living with myself. In return I can live and be of service to my fellow man. This is the purpose and reason behind writing this book. In order to live a life full of intimacy with my fellow man first I have to learn to live a life full of intimacy with Andre.

HOW COULD THIS HAPPEN TO ME?

It was early in the morning, around three am, on November 5, 2003. For some reason I had just awaken up to go to the bathroom. As I looked into the kitchen I saw nothing but flames everywhere. I attempted to reach the kitchen to use the phone to call the fire department. I was unable to reach the phone because the smoke was so intense and all I could think about was getting out of that apartment as quick as humanly possible. A few years earlier I had been diagnosed with sleep apnea. I had this large oxygen tank with a mask connected to it, which I use every night to sleep. I also carried oxygen around with me to breathe so I had around 15 oxygen containers in my bedroom that were full. Due to the amount of oxygen I had in my apartment, I had posters placed on the front and back door warning people of the danger of using fire around the apartment.

In the last ten years I had accumulated a sizable amount of awards, plaques, trophies, certificates and college degrees. They were displayed at various locations in my apartment. At the time of the fire material possessions did not seem to matter that much to me. All I could think of and focus on was getting out of that apartment. I remember trying to run out of the front door with one part of my pants on and trying to put the other part on while at the same time holding my sneakers and shirt in my hand. I remember seeing two of my neighbors in the back yard trying to fight the fire and yelling at them to get away because of the oxygen. I was heading down the end of the street when I saw the fire trucks and warned them of the oxygen.

That night I was taken to the local medical center for smoke inhalation. They suggested to me that I spend the night so they could run tests and make sure that I was alright. The next morning after I was discharged from the hospital I went to the apartment and saw that everything had been totally destroyed. I had lost furniture, important documents of myself and my deceased parents, and you could see the results of the fire everywhere you looked in the apartment.

That morning I spoke with the Fire Marshall and he told me that it was definitely arson and that the fire had been started from the back porch. I remember thinking to myself how could this happen. I know how it happened. The question that needed answering was why did I allow myself to get into a situation in my life where someone would want to take my life. What life path could I have taken to avoid this? The answer must lie within my life's story.

GROWING UP IN MY OWN SELF MADE PRISON

This story started fifty-two years ago in a small town in Central Jersey. My parents had migrated from South Carolina and Virginia to New Jersey. Due to the fact that my whole immediate family is deceased all the background information is coming from what I can remember and piece together and more importantly what God has allowed me to remember.

Before I start discussing my early childhood there is something I want to make real clear because it is very important. The person I eventually became had nothing to do with the examples shown me by my parents. They did everything they could to give me the benefits of what this life has to offer. My parents showed me a perfect example of a loving and caring couple. My father showed me how you treat women you claim you love with dignity and integrity. The ways that I eventually started treating women came from the examples I saw from my brother and those in the streets that I envied to be like and emulate.

My earliest recollections of my life as a young child has to do with my obsession of not being happy with myself and idolizing my brother. You have to understand that we were born eleven months apart. I can remember as a young child wanting to be like him and following my older brother around like a new born cub following its mother around. I remember once when my brother had started kindergarten my mother and myself had walked with him to school for his first day of class. It was only for half a day but I missed my brother so much. Later on that morning my mother was looking for me and was unable to find me. While she was searching for me she had a call from the school saying that I was up there. I remember my mother telling my father when he came home from work that night that she could not figure out how I was able to make it to the school by myself and cross the street and nothing happened to me. Another time my mother would take me shopping with her. She would buy me something such as candy or ice cream and I would keep it so that I could share it with my brother. As a young child I use to love watching the original Superman TV series, staring Steve Reeves. I would watch all the various super heroes shows but Superman was my favorite. I was so into Superman and his ability to fly and dealing with my feelings of low self-esteem and self worth that I would do things to get outside of myself so I could feel good about myself. One day I put my bathrobe around my neck and stood on the back of the bed and jumped off like Superman and pretend I could fly. One time when I was doing this I ended up hitting the opposite end bed frame and breaking my nose.

So as I continue to grow and age my desire to be like my brother intensified along with my desire for acceptance within my peer group. I recall we use to play this game where the guys would line each other's foot along side with the other person's foot and then take turns punching each other in the chest as hard as we could. The first person to move their foot back was considered someone with not having much courage of heart. Many days I went home in sheer agony from the punches because I wanted to feel a part of and not feeling that good about myself. We also played this card game called Knuckles. The number you would lose by was the number of times each participant would strike your knucles with a full deck of cards, which was 52. I remember going home many days with my knuckles swollen and bloody. I put myself through all this pain and agony just to belong and feel accepted. Also, during this period of adolescence I developed a lack of respect and understanding for the opposite sex. I remember we would pick out a certain female and then make monetary bets on how long it would take one of us to score on that individual. Now I see how we had basically reduced theses women to a piece of meat and not a human being.

At this time in my life while I was growing up one of the things that kept me imprisoned in my own self prison was the idea that I wanted to be considered more than what I really was. I remember my father would beat me for something I was told not to do and if I did not stop crying he would give me something to cry about. I remember after being beat a few times I told myself that I would never cry or allow anyone to see me cry. This attitude has followed me right into my present life. Even when my brother, father, and mother died I never shed a tear. I remember when I was in a drug rehabilitation center one of my counselors told me that I need to learn to deal with grief.

I need to say that at this time in my life as I was growing up I was developing certain beliefs concerning how one is to live their lives. I was brought up in my local church. I was a regular attendant of Sunday School and church services. A lot of values that I would lose and eventually regain later on in life were being instilled in me during this period of my growing up. But at the same time because I felt so bad about the person I was inside that once I was outside my home I would abandon those beliefs and values for those of the street.

I need to explain to you that I came from a pretty well off middle class African American family. I came from a family where there were two loving parents in it whose only concern was how they could live a lifestyle that would be for the betterment of their two young children and how they could improve the quality of their lives.. ***I DID NOT COME FROM A DYSFUNCTIONAL FAMILY.*** I recall hearing my parents at night sitting down at the kitchen table and discussing together with each other and valuing each other's input about what they were going to do in terms of raising my brother and myself. There was no spousal abuse or substance abuse going on in the house. I can not even recall times when there was liquor in the house. To show you the kind of people my parents were I remember I have an aunt who had moved to New York from South Carolina with her two young daughters. She was having a pretty hard time working and raising these two children. Even though she had three brothers it was my father who told her to come and live with us in the upstairs apartment of the house we owned. He told her to work and get herself into a position where she would eventually be able to stand on her own two feet. Eventually, she was able to move to Plainfield and purchase a house where she still lives in today. This is the kind of family I was born into. I remember my parents arranging their work schedule so that one of the parents was always at home with my brother and myself. You might ask yourself how could someone being raised into this type of family allow what happened to me happen. Many nights I have laid awake thinking the same question to myself. My father was very much into education even though he only had a high school education himself. I remember we had a black library in our house with all types of books describing what African Americans have contributed to the United States. So when in public school and certain people were given credit for inventing or discovering this or that inside I really knew who should be receiving the credit. My father also was heavy into church service and was a member of the local NAACP. So you can see I had all the benefits of life that a young individual would need to succeed in this life. It is just that I made a decision not to take advantage of it because what my brother and other people in the area were doing seemed more exciting and adventurous to me.

I remember right after graduating from junior high school my father sent my brother and myself to Lauringburg Institute in Lauringburg, North Carolina. It was a basketball camp where many young kids from the north who were aspiring to become professional basketball stars in their future had the good fortune to attend. I remember one individual named Charlie Scott, who later on went to find fame and fortune in the National Basketball Association with the Denver Nuggets. I remember so much wanting to be like him, shoot like him and even portray his personality. For the first time in my life I wanted to be like someone besides my brother and Superman, but not myself. I remember seeing him down there acting and treating people like he was better than everyone else there. I remember him going to classes whenever he felt like it and because he was so good in basketball he was able to get away with that behavior. It was here that I started to formulate the concept that if you excel at something then you can do anything you want. I mention this to let you know that I felt so bad about myself that it was easy to imagine that I was someone else. I remember thinking that since I was heavy set and not all that well nice looking like my brother I needed to do things that I personally did not enjoy doing just to be able to get outside of myself and feel that my life was somewhat worthwhile. Let me also say that at this time in my life that there was not always drama going on and that there were happy times also. Down in North Carolina I got my first opportunity to learn to ride a horse, but even doing that I did things to get outside of myself. I remember watching television at home and seeing how the Indians would ride a horse bareback and I decided that was what I wanted to do. I was told it was dangerous and warned against it, but in my mind I convinced myself that I could do it. Many times today when thinking of the things I allowed my mind to get myself into because of the misconception of the extent of my intellect I remember something one of my friends today always says. His saying was that *"He has a mind that he doesn't trust and a body that will follow."* I can't remember how many times that one sentence has lead me down in a downward spiral.

The following year my father sent me to Mather Academy in Beaufort, South Carolina. It was a private school in the south for African American youths entering high school. I remember when I arrived there I noticed that there was about four of us from the north. I also noticed the majority of the students down there treated us differently because of the preconceived ideas they had of us. These ideas were based on what they had read or heard of what goes on in the north. Once again I was in a position where I could get outside of myself and pretend to be someone else. I remember telling my father before I left that I didn't want to go mainly because it meant I would be away from my brother. Plus I would be forced to live and make decisions on my own. At home I was able to ask my brother if I should do this or that and when he responded to what I should do I didn't have to take responsibility for my own life and the mistakes I made in it. I remember down in South Carolina I was taking piano lessons and was real excited about it and couldn't wait to tell my brother about it. Upon telling my brother about it over the phone one night he sarcastically in his own way told me that only gay people or people who were eventually going to turn gay played the piano. He used Liberace as an example. Upon hearing this I immediately stopped taking piano lessons. I remember using the image that people had of people from the north to bully my way around. The one instance I can think of was when I was called into the principal's office and he had told me that he had been in touch with my father. My father had given him permission to do whatever is necessary to discipline me. At this time teachers were allowed to physically discipline students. At this time when the principal was preceding to tell me what he had intentions of doing to me I responded by reminding him where I was from. I also let him know that if he thought that I was going to quietly sit there and take whatever he planned to dish out that he was sadly mistaken. At this point the principal told me that he thought it would be best for everyone's concern if I went back home. Upon hearing this I was filled with joy because I knew I would again be around my brother, and I didn't worry about what my father would do to me for getting expelled. Many times I wonder what might have happened to my life if I had stayed down there for my four years in high school and graduated.

Upon my return to the north I was enrolled in the public school system. I was always good in the subjects that interested me. At the same time I noticed or it was my perception that my brother who did worse in school than I did was receiving more attention from my parents than I was. It wasn't until later in life that I realized that was not true and in reality it was the exact opposite. I was the one that was sent to a private school and not my brother. So I allowed my perception of things to influence how

I lived my life. I could never understand why my parents were so much harder on me in terms of schoolwork than they were of my brother.

I remember the time my father took me to Washington, DC to the March on Washington and heard Dr. King deliver his world renowned "The American Dream". I was so impressed with all the people that came down from different parts of the country to take part in that event. There were busloads of people who had taken off from work to take part in this march. Now there was someone besides my brother that I could try and emulate and be like, beside myself. I can recall times when my father had purchased a lot of Dr. King's speeches and sermons and I would practice repeating them in the house as if I was actually making them in person. I remember also being confused at this time. This was the time when the Muslims, Black Panthers and other militant black groups were growing in popularity and such people as Malcolm X, Eldridge Cleaver, Angela Davis, Huey Newton and Bobby Seales were making names for themselves. I can remember believing inside of myself the non violent concepts of Dr. King but once outside the house wanting to identify with the violent concepts of Malcolm X, such as "by any means necessary".

Still living in this self made prison I found myself acting out in ways that definitely was not the way my parents raised me. I can still recall the day when the announcement was made that the Rev. Dr. Martin Luther King, Jr. had been killed. The group of kids that I ranned around with had gotten together and decided that when we went to school the next day that anyone white that we saw we would beat up. It wasn't that I was upset about the fact of Dr. King's death but wanting to be accepted by my brother and the group we ran around in that I was willing to do anything to be accepted. I can remember acting one way and going home at night and feeling so empty and filthy inside for acting out on behaviors that I really did not approve of. It was also during this period of time that I had begun to formulate and put into motion my attitudes towards the opposite sex and many of them were derived from the way I saw my brother treat them. During my period of adolescence part of my self-esteem problems were derived from my physical appearance. I always considered myself overweight, not very intelligent, unattractive and living in my brothers footsteps. I watched how he always had girlfriends and never really treated them with any respect but for some reason or another they allowed that type of treatment to go on. I soon began to believe that was the way women wanted to be treated. These women were being treated not as a human being or someone to be respected but just as a piece of meat. I remember instances where my brother would tell women if they wanted to have anything to do with him that they had to take care of his brother, and they would. I started to think of women as unintelligent individuals. I remember some situations, which helped to formulate those beliefs. My brother would go with this one girl and every Friday he would have me drive him to her job and for one reason or another he needed money from her to fix this or that thing on his car. That would be the only time she would really see him until the following week. I use to think just how dumb can she be. I recall when she was having my brother's first daughter and he had me come to the hospital with him and watch her in labor. He found it very amusing and would remark that she doesn't look all that tough now. Even though I wanted to emulate him I couldn't because I just wasn't that cruel.

I remember that during this period of time in my life my parents would discipline my brother and myself and today their discipline might be construed as child abuse. I think my father was attempting to teach my brother and myself the right thing to do for the right reason and at this time the lifestyle being displayed on the streets was more attractive to us than what my father was trying to instill in us. I remember as a type of punishment was when my father would tell my brother and myself to stand on one foot and hold the other foot and we could not lean against the wall or table. He would sit there and make sure we didn't lean against the wall or table. He would have us do this for two or three hours. Many times our mother went to discipline us for something we had done. Since we were so much bigger and stronger than she was she would tie two or three extension cords together and wait until we were asleep and come into our bedroom and beat us until we woke up and disarmed her. I remember at this time as I was becoming bigger and older and strongerss when my mother would come to beat me I would just pick her up and sit her down and leave the house until she calmed down. I had gotten to the point when I would do something wrong and immediately go and tell my parents what I had done so they could give me my punishment and get it over with. At this point my parents were starting to realize that punishing my brother and myself was a waste of time because we would constantly do the same thing over and over again after being punished. I remember in my last year in high school my father finally got fed up with my brother and my behavior and went to the sporting goods store and bought some boxing gloves. He told us to put the gloves on and if we could beat him we could do whatever we wanted to around the house. I recall telling my brother to go first and since we were younger, stronger, and quicker he didn't stand a chance against us. After he knocked my brother down very quickly I was willing to allow him to run things the way he wanted to. At this time I was willing to go through any kind of pain as long as my brother was there going through it with me.

I remember thinking at this time how lucky I was to be alive. At this time in my life I was only drinking and I remember driving home one night and being in this town that I had never been in before trying to get home to the town where I lived. The next thing I had blacked out and the next thing I remembered was the police and rescue squad dragging me out of my van. The police had told me that I was lucky to be alive. Evidently, I had blacked out and ran my van straight into a telephone pole and the pole came down and split my van in half. Being in such denial I had completely blacked that out of my mind and it wasn't until I was writing this manuscript that I was able to remember that incident.

Still walking and following in my brother's footsteps when he decided to quit high school I followed suit. Even though it was in January of my last year it didn't matter to me. All I knew was that I wanted to be like and follow in my brother's footsteps. It wasn't until many years later that I was able to go back and receive my GED. When I made this decision my father also made a decision of his own. Either my brother and ss myself would join the service or go out and get a job. It seemed that joining the service would be the easier of the two. I thought that joining the service would make my life so easy. I figured getting somewhere to sleep each night, getting three meals a day; what else could anyone want. It wasn't until later that I realized that was the beginning of my downward fall.

THE BEGINNING OF MY DOWNWARD FALL

After quitting high school my brother decided to enter the United States Marine Corp. We talked about going into it together. At that time they had something called the buddy system. The buddy system was explained to us that my brother and myself could enter the military together and be assigned together. Our decision was that my brother would go into the Marines and upon graduating from basic training I would go into basic training and on my completion of basic training we would be assigned together. Well, when my brother came home from basic training and commenced to tell me how vigorous and demanding basic was I couldn't wait to get to the Air Force recruiter. Once again wanting to be like my brother and not believing I had what it took to follow through.

For the first time since my father had sent me to Mather Academy I found myself in a situation separated from my brother and having to depend on my own thinking. I spent a lot of time on the phone talking with him. I recall one instance when I was stationed in Colorado Springs and had just received my order to go to Thailand. At this particular time I was involved in my first romantic relationship. I need to point out here that when I picked this girl I was looking for the type of women I thought my brother would go out with. I was comteplating marriage and or course rather than call my mother and father to discuss it I called my brother. To me whatever my brother would say to me was an indication of what I needed to do. My brother proceeded to ask me if I was crazy or on drugs. He asked me what do I think she will be doing when I was over there thousand of miles away. Now keep in mind that my brother had never met or talked with this individual. My brother had convinced me that if I married her when I left she would be sleeping with every Tom, Dick and Harry. Upon hearing this advice from my brother I quickly put an end to that relationship. Once again I wonder what my life would have been like if I had went on my own feelings and not rely on my brother telling me how I should run my life. I also remember being stationed in Colorado and hearing all these stories from people returning from South East Asia and how exciting and adventurous they made it sound about doing duty overseas. So on a regular basis I would go to the headquarters office and continually request for overseas duty. It was at this point I learned about being careful of what you ask for because you might not be in a position to handle it. Plus, it just might not be in your best interest. Eventually, I received my wish and got my orders to report to Ubon Tani, Thailand.

Before I left for Thailand I took my leave. Instead of going home and visiting with my parents of course I did the only intelligent and reasonable thing I could do. That was to go and visit my brother, at Camp Lejune, North Carolina, where he was stationed. At the end of visiting with my brother I had received all the information I submised I needed to survive in a foreign country. Keep in mind my brother had never been outside of the United States and my father had served in various countries during WWII. Now I was ready to leave for Thailand.

I recall one of the first experiences when I arrived in Thailand. That experience had to do with my willingness to do anything to feel accepted because I never felt accepted within myself. I arrived in Thailand in the spring of 1970 and the first thing they tell you is to report to the headquarters of where you were being assigned. Well, I was a little hungry so I decided to find out where the chow hall was and get myself something to eat. I remember getting my tray and sitting down to eat by myself and some people coming up to me and asking me if I was new here and where was I from. When I told them I was from New Jersey they responded by asking me if I get high. Even though at that time in my life I didn't feel compelled to answer yes, just so I would be accepted into certain groups on base I told them yes. I left with them and went to another serviceman's apartment off base. I commenced to get high with these individuals that I had just met and had no knowledge of who they were. This was the beginning of my downward fall. I stayed all afternoon and night over there getting high. In the morning I had to report to my base headquarters and come up with a reason why I was late reporting. I can not remember what I told them but I do remember that was the beginning of my lying to cover up my substance abuse usage.

When I think of the fire at my apartment it is becoming clear to me how I ended up in that situation. I have heard a lot of people say that you do not realize how lucky and bless you are until you leave home and experience how other people are struggling to survive elsewhere. I think about the living conditions that I had to live in over there and how fortunate I am today that it just makes me sick to my stomach thinking of the opportunities that I have wasted away. I remember at first seeing the living conditions of the country and thinking this is what I volunteered for just to get some free drugs. I remember when other people over there were purchasing custom made clothes and ordering brand new automobiles to send back to the states I was wasting all my money on narcotics. I recall when some of the other soldiers would earn a three-day pass and would use it going to Bangkok for some s rest and relaxation. I would use my three days just smoking opium. I remember living with this Thai woman named Sumon. As I recollect on those experiences today I can understand how each of these events step by step led me into a course of self destruction that eventually led me into a house being set on fire. I remember how my self esteem and self worth and self acceptance was so low that I felt the only people that I was worthy of being with were prostitutes. I believed that their self worth and self-esteem was almost or more on a level equal to my own. I believed that they were not in a position to say no to me, especially when I was holding a product that they needed and did not have the funds to purchase themselves. So I found myself in Thailand and prostitution was a way of life for the women there. I remember thinking of being so grateful to the Air Force for sending me over there.

Going back to the woman I was staying with, I learned more from her about treating a woman as I had in my whole life in the United States. Over there in Thailand they had this communication system that makes our present system look very simplistic. I have witnessed cases where a serviceman might mistreat a Thai woman and within the space of an hour everyone knew about it. You would find yourself blackballed and regardless of how much money you had you were going to spend the rest of your tour alone. I found myself treating this woman the same way I would want my female relatives treated. This attitude would soon change once I arrived back home into the states.

Let me talk a little now about the Thai people and the living conditions they lived in and the influence and effect it had on me. You have to understand that this was the first time in my life that I had been outside of the United States. One of the suggestions I was given when I left Colorado was to learn their customs and traditions and incorporate them into my life. I did exactly that. I went out of my way to learn the language and respect their customs. I was living in this bungalow with Sumon and the rest of her family. At this time back in 1970 you was able to go to the market and for $5 buy enough food to last for a month. One of their customs was when you first enter inside your place of residence you must take your shoes off. I followed that tradition. I also at this time had a housegirl who was at my beckon call. When I came into the bungalow and took off my shoes and work clothes she would follow me around and pick these things up. My housegirl would wash my clothes and have them ready for the next day's work. She would also prepare my meals and bring them to me and also satisfy my sexual desires. You must understand that the woman in Thailand are raised from childhood with the one goal in life is how to please their man and bring more children into the world. There was no such thing as indoor plumbing where I was living. The way we got our water was the woman would carry these long poles with buckets hanging on each end of their shoulders and go down to the river and fill them up and bring them back to the bungalow. This is how you bathed. You wash yourself with soap and then use these cold buckets to rinse yourself off with. As I was getting entwined with the traditions and customs of South East Asia I found myself using drugs more and more. This woman I was living with had a brother who worked for the Thai police and he would give me drugs to smoke whenever I would ask him. You need to understand that over there everyone smoked. The police did not have a problem with it unless you were trying to sell it or ship it to the United States in order to make a profit from it. That is when you would find yourself in jail. That was always the one fear I had being imprisoned over there. The Thailand government really did not want you over there so if you found yourself in their prison and did not have someone from base to bring you food you were really in trouble. I had been told stories since they did not want us over there that they would not feed Americans.

At this time my work ethics and personal appearance was slowly disengrating. I was a sergeant and my work duty was that I was in charge of a supply warehouse. I had three airmen that I was in charge of and who worked for me in the warehouse. In the warehouse we stocked different parts that would go onto airplanes in order to keep them flying. Our airfield was mostly comprised of B-52's. I would find myself laughing when I would receive a letter form my mother and she would say how glad she was that the war was over, according to the President at that time. I would then tell her that I didn't know what war he was talking about but our planes would leave fully loaded with bombs traveling to Viet Nam in the morning and come back that night empty. Part of my duty in the warehouse was when a airplane technician would call the warehouse with the need for a certain part to get the plane back in the air we had to get the part to the flight line as soon as possible. In order to accomplish this we had what we called "priority time". Priority time means we had a specific time to find the part and get it to the flight line. Like I was saying my work ethic was getting worse and my using becoming more and more a problem, but at that time I thought I was just having fun. I would go to the warehouse early in the morning and give everyone their assignments and tell them if they needed me I would be at the NCO (non-commissioned officers) club. At the NCO club I found myself drinking and swapping drug stories with other comrades over there who found themselves living the same type of lifestyle as I was. I can recall many times getting a call and taking my time getting back to the warehouse to see what the problem was. Then I would have to lie or put the blame on one of the other men under my command for not having the part on the flight line on time. At the same time I was putting my life in more deadly situations. One such situation was since we had to get the part to the flight line by a particular time we had these trucks with the lights on top of them flashing. What I did on many days was fly around the base at unsafe speeds with the lights flashing with no place in particular to go. No one knew that and all they knew was that since the lights were flashing it was job related. I recall this game we would play with the trucks, in matter of fact it was two games. One was that we would go to the dirt roads at the back of the base and drive towards each other real fast from opposite directions. Then we would see who would be the first one to swerve off. That one would be considered less that courageous of heart. The other game was we would have someone in the truck with us and as we were driving at high speeds the person next to you would keep his foot on the gas pedal. The object of this was to see how long it would take you to put your feet on the brake. We would be doing all these insane acts while we were smoking more and more opium.

    I remember I had this one friend over there that was a pilot and was smoking as much as I was. This one time I questioned him about why he was smoking so much and then get into his B-52 and fly it each morning.

His reply was that I try flying to Viet Nam knowing you were going to drop bombs that were going to kill many innocent individuals. As far as he was concern no rational man could do that with the knowledge that they were going to kill many innocent, women and children that had done nothing to you. He confided in me that he just couldn't do that straight. I remember seeing accidents on the flight line where a plane would just burst into flames. I believe at this point in my life I started to formulate this concept of life that since life was so short and you never knew when your time was up that while I was here I was going to have as much fun as possible. I think this is why I found myself smoking more and in more death defying situations.

I recall how today I have seen movies and have heard stories about people playing Russian roulette with their lives and thinking how crazy and insane they were. Now I see how I was participating in that same behavior. By this I mean that when in Thailand I was seeing so many beautiful women from that part of the world that I had decided to sleep with as many of them as humanly possible before I returned back to the states. At this time I was still staying and sleeping with this one woman and my house girl. When I first arrived in Thailand I had to attend this course on base that dealt with the Thai people and their customs and traditions and how to survive over there. One of the things that was discussed as I mentioned earlier was that prostitution was a way of life over there. The women had to go to the clinic on a regular basis and get these cards saying that they had been checked out and that they were okay. At this time AIDS was not as well known and circulated as it is now. If you contracted something from one of these women you could always go back to the base and get a shot and refrain from sex for abut a week and then go back to our regular behavior and activities. With this knowledge in the back of my mind I was not asking to see anyone's card. I was just going from one woman to another and running back and forth from the clinic getting my shots. It is only through some force outside of myself that I did not contract anything.

When I first arrived in Thailand my feelings of self worth was very low. Then I met these women who would treat me like a king and I thought I had died and went to heaven. I recall one instance when I had went with Sumon to go to the river to get some water for the bungalow and on the way back I ran into one of my fellow servicemen from the base. Now mind you the way the Thai women transported the water from the river to their bungalow was by carrying these long poles with a bucket attached to each end of them on their shoulders. These buckets were full of water and were quite heavy. The Thai women showed their men very much respect. Sumon did this by standing behind me the whole time I was talking to my friend from base and did not say a single word until I had finished talking. Try that with some of these American women. So eventually I thought that I was in love or what I perceived to be love. Naturally, I wrote home to my brother telling him about Sumon and my intentions of marrying her and bring her back to the states with me. I do not know if it was my sex drive out of control or if the drugs that I had been taking were taking complete control of my sense of reality. Upon hearing this my brother wrote me back asking me if I had bumped my head or something or if I was totally out of my mind. Anyway, he convinced me that would be the biggest mistake of my life. So what did I do? I did what I always do and ended the relationship amd moved back to base.

While back at base I decided to just hang around the base for a while and try and get my senses back together. I remember this one guy from the south that would never leave the base to go into town with us. He always talked about his just getting married and was not going to do anything to put his marriage in jeopardy. I tried to convince him that he was crazy thinking his wife was being faithful to him. No matter what I said he held on to his own belief. Today, I can see that he was in love with his wife and for him it was more than just a physical act. I am seeing all these various things that were putting to an end my ideas and concepts towards my fellow man. In order not to think about it I dealt in drugs deeper and deeper. Eventually, they always say now God will do for you what you can not do for yourself. I guess God decided that he better get this fool out of here before he kills himself. The next thing I knew I had my orders to return to the United States.

THE FALL CONTINUES BACK AT HOME

My trip back to the states was almost the same except for one single item. On the way back I had stopovers in Viet Nam, the Philippines, Guam, Hawaii and California before I landed in San Antonio, Texas. The only thing different this time than when I left was that I hadn't drank or used any drugs before I left. The only reason behind that was that I had been warned by some of my fellow servicemen in Thailand. They were on their second tour of over there and warned me that once I returned to San Antonio I would have to go through this debriefing phase. This phase consisted of psychological and drug testing. The results of these tests would determine whether or not I would be allowed to remain in the service. Once again I told myself I had beaten the system. Upon receiving my orders to report to Griffiss Air Force Base in Rome, New York, I proceeded to leave for home for a two-week vacation to visit with my mother, father and brother.

As you can probably deduced so far by the way I felt towards my brother that I spent most of my time with my brother. At this time I was also able to manipulate my mother into buying me a car to drive up to New York. Manipulating my mother had become a very easy thing for me to do. I recall when my brother and myself was a junior in high school we decided to tell our mother that if we had to walk to school we would not go back to school at all. One day my mother took us to Pennsylvania and bought both of us cars. Even though my brother would give other people a ride to school I had to put locks on my tires and gas tank. I would not give anyone a ride to school. Trying to emulate certain people whom I felt was mean and cruel I felt that in order to be accepted I had to portray the same traits in myself. I recall in the winter when it would be cold and snowing I would drive past people real slowly and not stop and give anyone a ride. So when my mother bought me this car, even though for a while I had been living on my own and making my own decisions, when I was around my brother I felt the same way when I was growing up with him. I remember when I first got the car my brother asked me if he could test drive it and I said sure. He came back two days later. I was angry but said nothing because he was my brother. So after going through this type of ridiculous behavior for two weeks it was time for me to leave and head for Griffiss Air Force Base.

One of the things that I learned upon arriving at Griffiss was that I had the power to influence people. For once in my life people were following me rather than me following them. There was this one guy I met there who was from the south. His persona was that of an idea-enlisted serviceman. He would report to work on time, have clean and ironed uniforms, his shoes were so shiny you could see your reflection in them. His bunk in the dormitory was so perfect you could bounce an egg off it and it wouldn't break. I on the other hand was the complete opposite. After hanging around me for a couple of months it was evident of the change in him. Not only did I change the way he did things but had an influence on his thought process. This change was not for the better. It is easy to see now how my thought process was slowly but consistently deteriorating. I remember spending all of my paychecks on drugs. When I wanted to go into town and didn't have any gas I would go into the supply depot where I worked. I went there during the night and stole cans of dry gas to put into my car. I wasn't looking at the fact that I was destroying my car. All I was thinking about was that I had a ride into town.

At Griffiss Air Force Base I never had a problem with buying drugs. The Air Police, which were the military protectors of the base, were my major supplier. They would make a drug bust on base and some of them would keep the drugs. Then the ones with the drugs would sell the drugs themselves. Whenever I was in need of drugs I didn't have to risk going into town. All I had to do was go over to the Air Police barracks.

The nearest town to Grifffis Air Force Base was Utica, New York. Now in towns like Utica and most military institutions around the world the men who lived in these towns did not particularly like the servicemen.

They felt we were stealing away all of their women. It wasn't our fault that these men did not work and did not have any future to look forward to. With that in mind it is easy to understand how these men did not have anything to offer in terms of a future for the women there. I particularly did not care for them either. So the feeling towards one another was mutual. It had gotten to the point where it was not safe for the servicemen to go into town on the weekends alone. At this particular time I had made friends with this guy from New York whom also happened to be a black belt in karate. He taught a karate class on base. My interest in the martial arts did not just start here. It began when I was stationed in Thailand. I had signed up for kickboxing but after hearing the instructor and what he expected of us I knew that we would be separating company very soon. He expected us to do our job on base then report to his training facility where we would train and exercise for a couple of hours. On the first day he was telling us how we had to refrain from smoking, using drugs and chasing the Thai women. I instantly realized that his concept of training was going to interfere with the reason why I was there so immediately I made a decision to part company. So at Griffiss I found out that I could continue with the lifestyle that so much impressed me and also take martial arts lessons. The reason behind me taking these lessons was not so much to learn and understand the spirituality behind the martial arts but to be able to go into Utica whenever I wanted to by myself. I developed this relationship with my karate instructor. He happened to drink and use drugs as much as I was. We decided that we would go into town together on weekends since I had the means of transportation and I would begin arguments with the men of Utica and when they were about to jump me then my karate instructor would step in and take over. It had gotten so bad that I could only go into town when I had him with me. I remember one time I had asked him wasn't there a law that said he had to let these people know that his hands were registered as a lethal weapon. His response to me was that they would find out soon enough. For some reason I found that response amusing. At this time my substance use was increasing and it was having a profound effect on my behavior and personal appearance.

    To give you more evidence on how the drugs caused me to change internally I recently received a package of my military records from the National Personnel Records Center in St. Louis, Missouri. On my Airman Performance Reports I received 7 and 8's out of a possible 9. My commanding officers commenting stating that my strengths were that I was neat in appearance, courteous, and obedient at all times. He also remarked that my military bearing and dress on and off duty was such to bring credit to the Air Force and myself. He also stated that my attitude and enthusiasm gave me the potential of a career in the Air Force as a NCO. When I returned from Thailand it was as if there was a completely different person in the same body that left for Thailand. First, of all I did not complete my tour of duty over there due to my consistent drug use. Upon being stationed at Griffiss Air Force Base in Rome, New York I finished a Drug Rehabilitation Program, but I continued to use. Eventually I was dropped from a Sergeant to Air Man First Class with a substantial loss in pay but I continued to use. Then I was caught during an inspection with an ounce of marijuana in my locker and also showing disrespect to a noncommissioned officer, by uttering profane speech. At the same time I was counseled regarding drug involvement, traffic violations and duty performance, and given a Letter of Reprimand for failing to repair a detail formation at the required time. Eventually I had my driving privileges revoked to drive on base. Eventually, they got tired of my unwillingness to behave in the proper fashion and they gave me the option to leave the Air Force with an honorable discharge or go to trial and receive a dishonorable discharge and probably end up in a Federal Prison. I guess you can tell I took the honorable discharge. After doing all the necessary administrative paperwork to receive my discharge I found my way back home to New Jersey.

Once back at home I knew I needed to find a way to have some income. Before I left for the service I was working at this factory in another town and knew that there was a law that stated if someone left a job to join the service that job would be theirs when they returned home. I also knew that servicemen upon their release were entitled to draw unemployment insurance. That is what my brother was doing for income. At this particular time I had a cousin who was working in Washington, DC for the Justice Department. She had become disillusioned with the legal process and decided that she was moving to Los Angeles, California and asked my brother and myself if we would like to go there with her. Of course the answer was **YES**_ My cousin was the first one to leave. She drove out there and obtained the apartment. My brother flew out there next and I was the last one to fly out there.

All three of us was living in this one bedroom apartment and collecting unemployment. Our daily meals were consisting mainly of peanut butter sandwiches. Our goal was to party in Los Angeles for a year and when we got down to our last unemployment check we would fly back home. At this time we were also doing a lot of traveling. I remember us driving to

Los Vegas and Reno, Nevada. Since I have never been big on gambling I would spend most of my time watching my brother and my cousin gamble. So as we continually partied and traveled around we drew close to the time when we would be receiving our last unemployment check and would have to start arranging transportation back home. I wasn't ready to go home yet so I had found a job with this magazine crew that traveled around the country getting magazine subscriptions. The law says when soliciting magazine subscriptions door to door that when you arrive in a new town you are suppose to report to the local authority and purchase peddling permits. When you didn't get a permit the neighbors called the police when they saw strange people in their community and we usually ended up in jail until the company paid the fine to get us out. The magazine crew that I was working with decided that it was easier and cheaper to pay the fines and get us out of jail than to purchase permits at every new location. So I ended up going to jail in Los Angeles, San Francisco, Oklahoma City and Chicago. When I ended up in jail in Chicago the judge had decided that I would stay in jail for 30 days, instead of just paying the fine and moving on. At the end of my 30 days the magazine crew had worked its way to New Jersey. At this time I had gotten to the point where I was getting tired of going to jail. I contacted them and let them know it was time for me to be released and they sent me bus fare to come to New Jersey. I had decided at this time as soon as I arrived in New Jersey I would go home and that would be the end of my career with the magazine crew. That is exactly what I did.

Once I returned home I knew that I would have to find some kind of employment so I went on a journey to find myself work. I would constantly find small jobs here and there. At this time I would sell drugs to supplement my income. Also, at this time my aunt had rented me an apartment. I recall my father telling my mother that he did not know why I was living over there since my mother was constantly supplying me with dinner. I had liked the idea of having my own apartment because now I could use drugs whenever I wanted to without worrying about anyone catching me. One day I had left the front door unlocked and my father came over and saw this bag of marijuana on my living room table. I remember my father taking the bag and flushing it down the toilet and my brother asking me how could I let him just come over here and do that. I responded by telling him if he didn't like it then he should have said something. At this point in my life I really wasn't doing that much drugs. I had decreased the amount of drugs I usually would take and was more involved into making money. Also, at this time I was able to get a job which I would hold for the next eleven or twelve years.

Also, at this time my brother was involved with this white girl. I remember when we were living in California she would constantly fly out to see my brother and give him money for whatever reason he would come up with. It reminded me of how that other girl behaved. I was beginning to believe that it wasn't a race thing but that women in general were stupid when it came to relationships. I need to say that at this time I was under the illusion that most of my problems stemmed from the treatment I would receive from the white establishment. So sometimes when my brother would argue with this girl and ended up fighting with her I would sit there and watch him beat her up. I remember my mother questioning me on how could I just sit there and say nothing. My response was "you make your bed so you lie in it". Also, at this time I had begun to get involved in disco playing. It wasn't so much in the beginning my love for music but the extra benefits that go along with it. I started to notice that disco players would have groupies just like drug dealers. I had begun disco playing at a local bar where I lived. One of the side benefits was at the bar the owner would have go go girls dancing there from New York. At the end of the evening the owner would have me take them home to New York. As I started taking these girls home and they were becoming a regular at the bar we started to develop a friendly relationship. I recall a few times when I did not feel like driving to New York and they would stay with me in my apartment at my parent's house. Eventually it became a sexual relationship, and then when the owner decided to stop having dancing and switched her format to disco these sexual relationships came to an end. At this time I had become quite good in disco playing and had begun to buy my own system. I had begun to make a name for myself. I was being asked to play all over the state. Life was really worth living at this time. I had a good job making a nice salary, had my own apartment and was disco playing at the bar in the town where I lived. Money was really coming in and it was allowing me to buy more and more drugs. At first I mostly started drinking but now at this time it was predominately-snorting cocaine.

At this time I had been hired to play in this bar in Paterson every Friday, Saturday and Sunday, so I had to stop playing in Somerville. As I was playing in Paterson one of the regulars was telling me of two places people go in Paterson after the clubs closed. One place was an after hours establishment that were paying the police off to operate and you could go there and put your drugs on the counter along with your drink. You never had to worry about someone stealing your stuff when you went to the bathroom because everyone there had his or her own package. The other place was an after hours disco where people would go after they left the first after hours establishment to do some dancing before they went home for the night. Usually when I went to this place I would leave my drugs in my van hidden underneath my disco playing equipment. One night when I was there the police raided the club and had everyone lined up against the wall and was searching everybody. Those that had something on them were arrested and taken to jail but because I had left my stuff in my van I had once again beaten the system.

Everything that I was doing during this period of time was not inspired by the thought of how to continue using more and more drugs. While I was disco playing in Paterson for about three years I would play every year in their park for their annual community picnic which they had in an attempt to bring unity to the community. I played there for free and at that time that was a big deal because I lived more than an hour away. At that time I wasn't doing anything for anyone and if I did they were paying me. Consider having to load the van up with the equipment, drive for an hour, unload the equipment and set up the music. Then I had to play for about eight hours straight, then have to break down and pack up the equipment and drive home and then put the equipment back in my basement, and then do it all for free. For me that was a big deal or it was a way to validate myself because of the lifestyle I was living.

Eventually I lost my job at the plant factory because my conduct was not conducive for employment. Just like at Griffiss my attitude and behavior started to change for the worse. I would stay up all night drinking and snorting and then call myself going to work. I recall one instance when I came to work, was there about five minutes, punched back out and went to the first pay phone and called in sick. It never dawned on me that people had actually seen me in the plant that morning and had seen my jeep pull out of the parking lot. I had gotten to the point where I was bringing beer into the men's locker room during break and making liquor runs during our fifteen minute breaks. To top things off I was working in a chemical plant. I was a machine operator and I was dealing with some very dangerous chemicals. On certain occasions I would have to go outside and hook up rail cars to bring the material into the building. If the wrong chemical was hooked up that could have been the end of that town and all the neighboring towns.

I really did not care about losing my job because I felt that with the disco playing on the side I still would have plenty of money to take care of my personal business. Plus the working really was taking to much time and now I found myself with more time to devote to the thing I got the most satisfaction out of anyway and that was getting high. My disco playing was still going good. I was getting a lot of jobs around the state to go along with the regular Thursday, Friday, and Saturday's I was playing in Paterson.

Also, around this time I had started a relationship with this girl I met in Paterson, who would come around to hear me play. She informed me that she was a lesbian but had been known to go both ways. My self-centerness told me I did not really care what she did as long as she was available when I wanted to see her and do something, and that was always the case. I even turned her mother on to her first snort of cocaine and eventually her mother became a regular customer of mine. Whenever the family would see me they knew it was going to be partying time.

At this time in my life I was even involved in various entertainment activities. My addiction hadn't taken over complete control of my life yet. I would go to all the Knicks home basketball games. I remember being there when Larry Bird would come to play, when Michael Jordan would come there, when Magic Johnson was there, when Bernard King first came back from the injured list and when Julius Irving played his last game at Madison Square Garden before he retired. Because I was involved with music I was attending all the major clubs in New York at this time. I recall one year I had taken two females to a concert to see Ashford and Simpson at Radio City Music Hall and then went to spend New Year's Eve at their restaurant on 20th Avenue in Manhattan. I bought a bottle of Don Perone to show the girls how large I was living. I had even gotten into photography. I had bought me this camera with all the accessories that go along with it, including tripod and extensions, and was taking pictures every where I was going. Eventually, I had gotten tired of traveling back and forth to Paterson to deejay. The lady who owned the local bar in my home town called me up and told me she was having problems with the individuals she had hired to play disco there. So she decided she wanted to purchase her own equipment and then only had to find people who knew how to use the equipment. So she called me up and gave me a blank check to buy her a system and then hook it up. After the system was hooked up, she fired the other guy who was playing there and offered me the job again to play there.

DEATHS OF MY BROTHER, FATHER AND MOTHER

After I had hooked up the deejaying equipment system at the local bar I did not take the job of playing there immediately. I wanted to continue free lance playing for a while, but I also wanted to limit my traveling. At the same time I was becoming more involved and known for my music. It was becoming more of a career and love than it was when I first started. When I first started it was mostly for the money and the side benefits that came with it, which was the female groupies. I had a friend who was the local deejay of a local radio station and he would frequently have me down at the radio station where he worked at. This increased my base of people who were looking for deejays. I was still living at my apartment and to supplement my income I was selling more and more drugs at the same time using more drugs.

My brother was becoming more and more of a fixture at my apartment. He knew I always had drugs and would never charge him for them. He knew he could come over and get high for free. At this time he was still involved with that white girl and was bringing her over my apartment more and more. I didn't want her over there but I said nothing because he was my brother. I remember at this time one of my relatives had come over and was telling me how I had everyone fooled. I was told that if my parents ever found out how I was living and what I was doing they would have a heart attack. My brother had openly admitted to our parents that he used drugs but I was the perfect one. Also at this time I was a regular at my local church. The only thing that I felt I had missing in my live was the absence of someone from the opposite sex in my life. It seemed so unfair to me that everyone around me seemed to have someone in their lives and I had no one, but when they wanted drugs then I was the popular one and the one that everyone came to. I even realized that a lot of women that would come over there were putting aside their true feelings towards me in order to get high for free. Because my feelings of myself was so low I was willing to do anything to have people around me and have me thinking that I was the man.

My brother had this habit of getting good jobs but they never lasted. I do not know whether it was because of his drug addiction or his sex addiction but he was constantly losing these good jobs. So at this time he had gotten a local job in town. This one night he had come over to my apartment and he had just had a fight with his girlfriend and we had been getting high all night. In the morning he was late for work so he took a shortcut to his job by way of the railroad tracks.

The next thing I remember is I had received a phone call from my parents from the hospital telling me I need to get up there as soon as possible. When I arrived at the hospital my parents were attempting to explain to me what had happened but was having a hard time doing it. To sum everything up evidently a train had hit my brother on his way to work on the railroad tracks. When they asked me why was he up there I told them that was a shortcut to his job. I omitted the part of him being over my apartment getting high all night and was late going to work and that was a shortcut for him. For years I kept that guilt inside of me and dealt with it. Every since I was small and my father had told me if I wanted to cry he would give me something to cry about I had made up my mind then that noone would ever see me cry again. Every since then and up to the present I have never cried. Plus, I realized that I had to be the strong one now after seeing how hard this was affecting my parents. Then I was told to do the hardest thing I ever had to do. The doctors had told my parents that my brother didn't have that much time left and they felt that someone from the immediate family should be in there with him. They didn't believe that either one of them was strong enough to do it so they asked me to do it. I agreed to do it.

Nothing in my life that I had went through had prepared me for what I was about to face next. I walked into the room and what I say next was devastating, but I knew I had to be strong. I had to be strong not only for my brother and myself but also for my parents. There was blood and tubes and lines hooked up every where. They had to amputate one of his legs. I haven't had to deal with that image until recently when a friend of mine up here had one of her leg amputated, and that vision of seeing my brother like that came back. He was still semi-conscious and while I was next to him he whispered to me to take care of our parents and his two daughters. It wasn't too much longer that he passed away.

The next thing was to make preparations for the funeral. I was involved with every aspect of the funeral. This experience would serve me later on when my father and mother died and I had to make all the necessary preparations for their funeral. I was with my parents when they went to the funeral home to pick out the casket, go to the church and make the arrangements. I helped with the obituary and decide on how the funeral at the church would be. At this particular time I was sticking around the house because there was a lot of activity inside the house with people coming over to offer their condolesenses. My niece from North Carolina came up with her mother and at this time she wasn't old enough to understand what was going on. During this period I had refrained from using drugs but every time I went to the local bar in town everyone was buying me drinks.

A lot of pressure was being put on me. The night before the funeral when the body was laying in the church for people to view I was told that someone from the family should be there. Once again I had to be the strong one. The day of the funeral I had to be at the church early and sit with the body. I was amazed at the amount of people that came out to pay their respects to my brother. I remember thinking if that many would show up for my funeral. Then when everyone was making their last trips to view the body before it was closed I put a bag of marijuana in it when I went past. I stood chose to my parents during this period of time. When I found myself alone I found myself withdrawing deep inside of myself. I feared having to face life alone now without the person I valued most in the world to be around me to advise me in what directions I should go in living my life. In addition I had to deal with the fact that I was blaming myself for my brother's death and not being able to share this information with anybody.

During the period right after my brother's death my father asked me to move back home. I had my things packed and moved back home that very same day. After the funeral my niece from North Carolina had stayed a couple of weeks to visit with my parents. I really paid her no attention because the reminder of my brother was too painful for me. That behavior continued well into this present day. I remember one day my father was watching her and he had to go to the store for a few minutes. My father told me to watch her until he returned back from the store. When he came back she was standing in the middle of the room that separate the kitchen from the living room, the same place he had left her at. Immediately he asked me what I had done or said to her and I told him I had did nothing to her. I did exactly what he had told me to do. He told me to watch her and that was what I did. I told him he said nothing about speaking to her or anything. It was during this period of time that I decided to take the job at the local bar deejaying.

During this time I was getting more involved into selling drugs and using narcotics. My usage increased because it was becoming increasingly easier to live in this imaginary world rather than live in reality and deal with the realization that I was responsible for my brother's death. My addiction had not become obvious to anyone around me so I was able to continue in this lifestyle for the next six years until my father became ill. I was still going to church and functioning in society.

Before my brother's death my parents had worked and invested their money successfully. They really believed that the best investment was in real estate. My father had found two houses in a neighboring town that he was considering purchasing for my brother and myself. Still not wanting to be far away from my mother I pronounced to them if my mother wasn't moving, neither was I. After realizing that his original plan was not going to work my father went on and purchased just one of the houses. It was during this period of time, a few years after my brother's death that my parents decided to move into the house they had purchased. Still trying to make things better for me my father had become involved in trying to be a store owner. I can recall going to New York with my father when he went to buy various merchandise to stock the store with. My father was working at this factory where he had been employed for many years. As long as I can remember he had been working there and he had also gotten my mother a job down there. My two other uncles also worked there. The store was not making money so my father decided to get out before he ended up in debt. For the next couple of years things were great at home with my mother, father and myself. It was during this period of time that my involvement in deejaying had reached the point where I had bought my own equipment. I had my equipment set up in the basement. I was spending more and more time in the basement practicing and playing. This would allow me the opportunity to stay within myself and not to focus on how my brother died. It was also during this period of time my parents were attempting to bond with their granddaughter. From time to time they would have her up here from North Carolina. My attitude towards her did not change because the more I looked at her the more I would see my brother. It was also during this time that my mother helped me buy a van so I could get around deejaying.

Approximately five years following my brother's death my father started experiencing heath problems. Most of his problems were based on his attracting asbestos from the plant where he was working. The asbestos was beginning to have effects on his heart. About a year following the beginning of my father experiencing health problems he passed away from a heart attack. I recall during the period of his illness he was retired from his job and was spending most of his time at home in the bed.

Once again I found myself in a situation where I had to be the strong one. My father's death really hit my mother hard. I remember being in the hospital with my father before he passed and him telling me that I would have to take care of my mother. I believed at this point that he knew he was getting ready to die. When this happened the only thing I could think of was what have I done so horribly for God to do this to me. First, my brother was taken away and now my father. I knew now I couldn't dwell on my own personal hurting because I knew at least until the funeral was over that I had to be there for my mother. Also, at this time my behavior and things I would say to people were unpredictable. I remember one night before the funeral our church's pastor had come to the house to see my mother. When he was ready to leave I remember hearing him ask my mother where I was. She told him that I was in my room not bothering anyone. She warned him that if he goes in there messing with me that she would not be responsible for whatever I might say or do. After giving that a second thought he changed his mind and went on home.

During the week before the funeral I found myself once again involved in all the planning for the funeral. I had to participate in going to the funeral home and picking out the casket. We had to select the suit my father was to buried in and then meet with the pastor to discuss the planning of the funeral. Like with my brother's funeral someone from the family needed to be down at the church during the wake. I knew my mother would not be able to handle that so I found myself once again sitting down in the church with the body for the entire wake. Like with my brother's death, I didn't cry at my father's death. This would be instrumental because years later I would find out that one of my problems stemmed from the fact that I never learned how to deal with grief.

Before my brother died my father bought a family plot for all four of us to be buried in together. This would be the first time since my brother's death that I had returned to the graveyard. The morning of the funeral I had to get up early and leave to be at the church when they opened the doors for the funeral. Again I was strong and there for my mother, but I wasn't there for myself. I was withdrawing deeper and deeper inside of myself. Like during my brother's death I had stopped using drugs and drinking for the period while the funeral was going on. My mother was from Virginia and all her relatives from there had came up to support her. I knew they were not up here to see me and I really did not want anything to do with them. I made my feelings through my behavior quite clear and obvious how I felt about them. One of my cousins stayed up here a week after the funeral to be with my mother. I knew she wasn't staying to be with me. I knew my mother was real disappointed with the way I treated them but I really did not care at this time. If things going on were not going to benefit me positively I was not interested in it. I remember at the grave site they were having the final services for my father. My niece was standing behind me along side with my cousin. I remember hearing her ask my cousin if she knew where my brother was buried at. My cousin responded that she didn't know where he was buried. The one person who knew where he was buried at was not asked. I was not going to volunteer the information that she was standing along side it. Later on I told my mother about it and once again she expressed her disappointment in me and asked me what in the world was wrong with me.

It would be a period of nine years after my father died that it was just my mother and myself. I was still deejaying at that same bar but I was also spending more and more time in my basement practicing my music playing. I was becoming more and more involved in drug selling and withdrawing deeper and deeper inside myself. I was starting to have relationships with various women but they were all drug related. All of these women were using drugs and if they wanted me to support their habit they were going to have to do things to make me happy. At this time I was starting to do things to people, not caring what the results would be, as long as I was getting what I wanted. I remember this one girl whom I had went to high school with was a pregnant and using drugs. I knew she was due to have her child any time and she had contacted me about buying some drugs. I sold her the drugs and rationalized to myself that if she didn't get the drugs from me she would get the drugs from somebody else. Using that rationalization I convinced myself that it might as well be me who got the money. This behavior was becoming increasingly more consistent and I was finding myself doing more things to cause pain to other people. I was doing all this while at the same time not caring about the harm I was causing as long as I was benefiting in the end.

    It was during this period of time that my using was starting to get out of control. I would go to a local motel and rent a room for four hours so I could smoke in peace and not have to share my drugs with other people. I had been making what I perceived as friends with people in town who were running crack houses just so I would have somewhere to go to smoke. Eventually, I was able to go over there when I had no drugs and they would turn me on for free. When at home I would still go in the basement to practice my music and a lot of times I would use that as an excuse to go down there and smoke. Eventually, I got caught down there and my mother was speechless. I decided to stop smoking around the houses but I needed to find a way to satisfy my desire to smoke. I came up with this brilliant idea, or so I thought it was brilliant, to get myself a room down the other end of town and I would be able to smoke as much as I wanted and whenever I wanted.

    During this time I gave my first fashion show. It was a success. I had my friend from the local radio station to act as MC and he gave away some tickets for me on the radio. I had hired models and was able to get stores to donate some of their clothes for the publicity they would receive in return. I had hired a music band to play and I was able to get a friend of mine who was a karate expert to give karate demonstrations. I played the music for the fashions show and dance myself. During this time I had become involved with this girl from Elizabeth. The way that I had met her was kind of unusual. Previously, I was staying with this one girl that I knew there was no future for me with but it was just something to do to help the time go by. I remember my cousin telling me she had read somewhere that if you bring in the New Year with a certain individual that meant you would be with them for the coming year. I knew I had no plan of staying with her for the coming year so five minutes before New Year's I walked out of her apartment and didn't come back until another hour. When I came back and she questioned me about why I left I lied to her about why I left and where I had went. About a month later a friend of mine whom I had worked with at the chemical plant had introduced me to some women in Elizabeth. The first relationship went no where because it was just a sexual attraction that was brought on by the fact that I sold drugs. The next one was completely different. This female I had met did not do drugs and she only drink when she was out at a bar or club. She had a regular job and was different than any other woman I had met. I need to mention that at this time that when I became involved with a female I would always ask myself if this is the same kind of women my brother would go out with. Even after my brother's death I was seeking his approval.

This woman treated me with more respect than I had become accustomed to. She would come to the bar where I was playing and if some man asked her to dance she would always ask me if I mind. I would tell her to go ahead because I knew at the end of the night she would be going home with me. Everyone would ask me how was I able to get someone as fine as she was. I was really starting to develop strong feelings for her and this was really scaring me. I was not sure if she liked me for what I could provide for her or the person I was. We continued to see each other for over a year. I remember she came down on my birthday and took me out to dinner. At this point I had advanced from snorting cocaine to smoking crack. Like in the past I figured we would come back to my room and she would stay for a little while and then proceed to go home. Before she got there I had purchased my crack and assembled all the various utensils I needed to smoke my crack in a little cabinet I had by my bed. Unknown to me for the first time she had planned to spend the night. After being there for a little while she was making herself comfortable and I was asking her how long she was planning on staying. After a while the compulsion to use had become so great that I pull out my stuff and started smoking. Immediately she told me that she had thought that was what I had been doing and that I needed to make a decision. That decision was whether or not I wanted to be with her or the drugs, but it wouldn't be both.

In the midst of my using I was supporting myself by getting jobs with various temporary agencies. Since I only had to pay rent for my room I was making enough money to support my drug habit. I really didn't worry about food because I knew I could always go to my mother's house and get something to eat. While I was living in this rooming house I came up with another brilliant idea. That idea was when I got paid on Friday's I would mail myself money orders for the following week ensuring that I would be able to smoke every day of the week. That idea never came to maturity. By Saturday morning I would be broke and would call my aunt, who worked at the local Post Office, and tells her that there was a letter for me and I would be coming by to pick it up. I would pay my rent by putting it in an envelope and placing the envelope in a slot in the landowner's office. I found myself on weekends trying to break into the landowner's office to get my check so I could purchase more drugs. I never worried about getting evicted because I knew that if I was evicted I could always go home.

After my breakup with the girl from Elizabeth I found myself smoking more and selling less. At this point I found myself becoming more involved with prostitutes and purposely going out pursuing them. My new playground had become New York and Elizabeth. At this time I was also hired and under contract with this modeling agency. I had been hired to do all the arranging and playing of music for their fashion shows. These shows were held in large, eloquent hotels and the money I was making was extremely good. This new source of income allowed me to dwell deeper into the lifestyle that I was having a real love affair with. I was going out with various girls in Elizabeth one after another and starting to get back into the drug selling business. I found out if I bought my drugs in quantity from New York I would make more money and would have some left over for myself. My driving route to New York was always the same and on the way home I would always stop in Elizabeth. I had to let all the women there know what a big man I was and how many drugs I had just purchased. My trips to New York were becoming twice a week occurrence. This one time on my way back from New York I stopped by this bar in Elizabeth and was dropping a friend of mine off at home.

Unsurprisingly, I was being followed and was surrounded and busted by the police. I was arrested, locked up in jail and my van taken. It took a few days for me to drum up the courage to call my mother and let her know where I was. At this particular time I was suppose to be doing a fashion show for the modeling agency. The lady in charge of the fashion show was constantly calling my mother asking her to get me out. At first my mother was not going to get me out and then later she did. When she got me out she let me know that it was for only one reason. She told me when my brother would get in trouble they would get him out so she felt it was only fair that this time she get me out.

I went to court and the prosecutor told me he would give me a good deal. He told me if I pleaded guilty to possession with the intent to distribute he would recommend that I get 365 days in the county jail. I knew that since I didn't sell drugs in Elizabeth he couldn't prove the distribution charge, so I turn down the offer. The prosecutor sent it to the grand jury and they refused to indict because he couldn't prove the distribution charge. When I went to court the judge asked me if I did not sell drugs to explain to him why I had so many drugs on me. The only thing I could think of to say was that I have a drug problem and when I use I do not like to have to keep running back and forth to buy more drugs. I further told the judge that when I was planning on getting high I would go to New York and buy me a large quantity of drugs to avoid all that running back and forth. For some reason the judge bought it and told me I needed to go into a rehabilitation center. He told me that while I waited for a bed to become available at the center he would place me on pre-trial intervention. Pre-trial intervention meant that if I stayed clean and out of trouble for a year the charges would be wiped from my record. That same weekend I was busted again in Elizabeth and when I went to court I was taken off pre-trial intervention. I had to go into the rehab immediately to avoid doing jail time.

When I first arrived at the rehab I found myself having a real hard time because I really did not want to listen and comply with the rules and regulations they wanted the clients to do. Many of my personal feelings were exactly that personal. Being that they were personal I did not want to share them with others. It wasn't until they made it clear to me that I was about to be kicked out and would have to go back to court and spend my sentence in jail that I was willing to listen. It was during my time here that I met this guy from Plainfield, who would eventually become good friends with me, even until this present time. After graduating from the program I was sent home to stay with my mother in Plainfield.

Before I continued more with my downward fall from reality I need to also state that at this time everything was not all that bad in my life. There were times that I did some good things. These times didn't outweigh the negative aspects of where my addiction had taken me. I remember my friend I met at the rehab was living with this girl and she had thrown him out when he relapsed. One day I saw him walking down the streets of Plainfield and asked him how he was doing and where he was going. He told me what had happened and that he was on his way to the local soup line. I told him let me talk to my mother and see if I could help him. My mother agreed to let him stay at our house and help get him back on his feet. The only provision was that he goes to these twelve step meetings with me and does not use any drugs. It was during this time that I started going to these twelve step meetings. I was attending these meetings but not taking them seriously and eventually I started using again and going back to my old lifestyle.

Going back to my old lifestyle involved me running around Elizabeth again. As I was running around in Elizabeth I ran into this guy referred to as New York. I think he was called that because he was crazy and unpredictable like the city. As I became more involved with him and his lifestyle I found myself wanting to be around him because people in Elizabeth were fearful of him because of his unpredictability. Eventually we developed a trust and bond in one another. Mine being around him gave me some sort of feeling of invincibility and was willing to take unusual chances. One time he asked me to take him to New York to purchase some drugs. He told me he would be in and out. What a surprise I had in store. After an hour of waiting I saw him come running down the street with people running behind him shooting. He had robbed these dealers. Talk about being scared to death. I got to New Jersey as soon as possible. He was shocked that I had waited for him. He had remarked that anyone else would have long been gone. I told him since I brought him out there I would bring him home. I guess I proved myself that night, because the next day he took me shopping and bought me some clothes. That afternoon he took me to a house of prostitution and told me to pick out any girl I wanted. Later on he showed me where he sold his drugs and announced to them that I would be making his pickups for him. I didn't have to ask him for drugs because he would just give them to me. I really was impressed with what I perceived was respect, but I know now it to be fear. I was impressed with how people responded to him. I found out that I could talk tough to some of these people and they wouldn't do anything to me for fear of his reprisal. He was so unpredictable. One night I was the victim of a hit and run. I do not know if it was an accident or it was purposely planned, but I wasn't hurt that bad. I was standing outside a bar talking to this guy when the next thing I knew I saw these headlights and people screaming. Eventually, my friend had gotten arrested with an attempted murder charge and went to jail. I had to stop coming to Elizabeth for a while because I had no one to hide behind or to protect me.

During this time period I had moved back home. I was still working for these temporary agencies and playing my music in my basement cellar. One day my mother went for her doctor's appointment and when she came home she told me she had been diagnosed with lung cancer. She had worked many years at the same place where my father had worked and contracted asbestos. My mother was not sure if her condition was due to the asbestos or that the many cigarettes she smoked. What amazed me was the fact that when she was given this news she stopped smoking that day until her death. My mother was told that she needed to take chemotherapy at a local rehab hospital, so I had to take her there five days a week for six months. In order to do this I had to have my license restored. When I had went to court earlier and in accordance with the laws of New Jersey my license had been suspended. When my suspension period was over my license stayed in suspension because I did not have the money to pay the surcharges. In order for me to take my mother to the hospital she gave me around $3,000 to pay off the surcharges. Once again my mother had bailed me out of a situation I had gotten myself in. Unknown to my mother and myself she had went to the doctor to late because the cancer had already started spreading. At this time I started drugs more and more, even though at this time I hadn't decided to stop attending these twelve-step fellowship meetings. Most of the time when my mother came home from chemotherapy she was too tired and weak to do anything but to go to her room and rest. Therefore I had to do everything around the house. I had to do all the cooking, cleaning, washing of clothes, food shopping, and taking care of the yard outside. I need to say at this time, unknown to me, when my father had died that my mother has sued the company he had worked with for contributing to his death and had won the lawsuit and had received a large sum of money. We had a large combination safe in the house and for some reason, which I do not fully understand, my mother kept the money from the lawsuit in there. My mother's other money she kept in the bank. For the next six months my mother continued to get continually worse. Near the end of the six months I remember going to the doctor's office with my mother and the doctor telling us that he wanted to operate to remove the cancer. My mother asked me what I thought she should do. After the doctor told us the positive and negative aspects of operating I wasn't thrilled with having the responsibility of making that decision. I remember telling my mother that if this is what the doctor is recommending then maybe she should go ahead with it. She agreed to the operation and the date was set. I was still attending the twelve-step meetings but I decided that this was something personal. I decided not to share and ask for help from the people from the fellowship.

The operation took longer than expected because the doctor ran into some unexpected problems. The cancer had spread and they had not counted on that happening. The whole time I was in the waiting room by myself. When my mother finally came out of the recovery room she had all these tubes and lines attached to her. It was like seeing my brother in his deathbed all over again. For the first time since I was a little kid I broke down and started crying uncontrollably. My mother was worried about the drugs and me so she had my aunt and a family friend come to the house and remove all the money from the safe, or so they thought. After they finished counting all the money and taking it with them I decided to clean out the safe. When cleaning out the safe I found one stack of hundred dollar bills that they missed. I couldn't wait to get to New York. In order not to think about what was going on I got myself a room at a motel for a week. I had this prostitute with me and no one knew where I was. After a week I found the strength and courage to go back to the hospital to see my mother. I could see in her eyes that she was disappointed in me and had given up on life. One day at home I received a call from the hospital to come up there as soon as possible. When I arrived at the hospital my mother had passed away.

Once again I found myself in a situation where I had to put my own feelings aside and take care of the responsibilities of planning the funeral. I recall at the hospital after my mother's death I ordered a biopsy and knew the doctor's were nervous about my reason for having this done. I think maybe deep inside I was looking for someone to blame for my mother's death so I could take the guilt from myself for advising her to have this operation. Once again I felt responsible for the death of two of my closest family members. I remember at this time making a promise to myself that I would never again allow myself to get close to anyone else so I would never have to go through this kind of pain when they leave. I was still using at this time but knew I had to keep everything under control at least until after the funeral.

At this time I was ready to stop attending those twelve-step meetings. I would go there during the planning of the funeral process but soon after the funeral I would completely stop attending those meetings. I did not want to share my pain with anyone. I chose to deal with my pain by using more and more. I convinced myself that the more I used the less time I would have to think about the pain and guilt I was dealing with.

I remember running around and doing the necessary things for the funeral. At the same time I found myself not wanting to be around or have anyone around me except for my cousin. She was the only one who knew about my return to using and promised me that she would not tell anyone. It was my cousin that convinced me to call my mother's relatives in Virginia and her granddaughter in North Carolina and inform them of the funeral plan. I had planned not to contact them. My behavior was so erratic at this time that people were nervous and cautious about coming around to see me. I remember my cousin telling me this was the first time she had been around the passing of someone where the grieving family had to buy their own food. At this time people would have friends and family members making sure they had food to eat. They knew that the grieving family would have so much on their minds and things to do preparing for the funeral that the least they could do was make sure the individuals did not have to worry about eating. For the first time I was able to get high in the house and I was taking advantage of this golden opportunity. When someone ranged the doorbell I was able to look from a window upstairs. I was able to see who was down there without them seeing me and if they were empty handed I wouldn't answer the door. It didn't matter to me whether they were family members, friends of my mother or church members. When my mother's sister came up with her sons I let my aunt stay there but told her sons they had took somewhere else to stay. I also told them they couldn't smoke cigarettes on the property. I remember my cousin from Virginia coming up but had to leave to go home before the funeral but had warned my aunt's sons about me and not to speak to me if I didn't speak to them. I remember one of them approaching me and telling me that they did not like the idea that I did not let their mother have any part in the planning of the funeral. I told them that this was a dictatorship and that the person that was paying the cost was making all the decisions. I also told them if they didn't like the way I was handling things that the highway that brought them up here runs the same way to take them home. When they went back home they told my cousin about it and she told me that she told them didn't I warn you and tell you not to speak to him if he doesn't address you. After the funeral I told all of them they had no reason to come back up here now since my mother was no longer here.

When my niece and her mother arrived they had to find a motel to stay in because I wouldn't let them stay in the house. I have an aunt that is always telling me that I should be good to everyone all the time, but my cousin who was more like a sister to me told me she would be happy if I just stay good till after the funeral. I remember her telling her mother that while my mother was alive she kept me some what in check and now heaven help them because there was no one to stop me from doing what ever I decided to do.

I remember the morning of the funeral the limousine arrived and I had planned to just let my cousin and myself ride in it. My cousin had convinced me to let my niece ride in it but I definitely would not let my niece's mother ride with us. My mother's sister wanted to ride with us with her sons but I told her she could ride but her sons could not. She decided to ride to the funeral home in another car with her sons. On the ride to the funeral home I remember my cousin telling me she couldn't believe how strong I was. Everything I have gone through seems not to bother me. I remember telling her not to believe everything her eyes see. She was referring to the fact that last night at the wake I sat down there with the body the whole time. Now I was going to the funeral. I went through the funeral, went to the grave site and was ready to go home. Everyone was telling me I should go to the church for food and refreshments and because people wanted to offer their condolescenes to me. I could care less what other people wanted me to do or say but I went so I would not have to constantly hear these people's mouth. After the funeral was over I was able to go home and the other people could go back to their lives. Now they could leave me alone and I could get high without people bugging me.

TWO YEARS OF UTTER DEGREDATION

It was during this time period that I completely stopped going to those twelve step meetings. I was still working at the temporary jobs but that was about to come to a close. In my mothers will there were provisions made to take care of me for the rest of my life. I had somewhere to live and was receiving income each month. It was during this time that my life went from just plain using to get high to sheer utter degradation. It was also during this time that I had been attending this outpatient program and when I left the program I convinced one of the girls there to leave and come live with me. Since she had no formal educational training she made her money by prostitution. That didn't bother me as long as I was beneifiting from her trade.

After I had stopped attending the twelve step meetings some of the people that I had met at the twelve step meetings were concerned about me and were coming around to see me. I would never let them in and told them that they shouldn't be coming around people like me, before they end us using again themselves. I had decided that I had no intention of stop using and I didn't want people around me that were going to try and persuade me to stop using. Eventually, they realized that they were wasting their time and they stopped coming around.

When you think of the two-year period it sounds like a long period of time. In reality as I look back on it the time really went by pretty fast. Not only did the time go by pretty fast but also the degradation and deterioration of my physical, mental and spiritual being went by just as fast. My moral values were changing. Things that my parents had taught me as a young child and the things that were taught me in church went out the window just as fast. I remember at this time I was still selling to supplement my income with the money I was receiving from my mother's will, but for some reason I was still going to church. I would go to church and have a certain amount of drugs on me. I knew I had planned to sell them when I got out of church. I did not want to take the chance of hiding them outside and someone finding them. Therefore, I kept the drugs on my person while in church. I wasn't going to church every Sunday and eventually I would stop going to church all together. Like every thing else I felt it was interfering with the time I could be selling and using drugs. Eventually the selling became less and less and the using more and more. Then when the selling came to an immediate halt I found myself willing to do anything to myself or anyone around me to continue using.

I remember my mind starting to play games with me. I remember sitting in the kitchen getting high and the kitchen lights would start blinking of and on. I was thinking that my mother was sending me a signal. My cousin had stopped coming around the house and told me one day that she always loved me but now didn't like the person I had become. The lack of respect I showed myself and especially women. I couldn't let what she thought of me get in the way of my continual using. I was becoming more and more involved with prostitutes. I would buy myself a certain amount of drugs then I would go out on the prowl for prostitutes. The girl that was also living with me could not satisfy my sexual desires, just like my appetite for drugs was increasing more and more.

It was during this time I met this guy who would eventually become real good friends with me. He sold drugs but he didn't use them so when he would come back from New York he needed someone to test his product to let him know if it was good or not. He would always give me a little for myself. I thought I had died and went to heaven. For him it wasn't always about the drugs. He would come over to the house and first ask me if I had eaten or not. If I answered in the negative he would take me out to eat before he gave me any drugs. It is easy to see how the using was effecting my mental and spiritual being. I also need to let you know it was affecting me personally as far as taking care of my physical body. I suffer from a second disease called diabetes and at this time was taking insulin three times a day. One day when I went for a doctor's appointment my doctor told me that it was dangerous for me to take insulin and drugs at the same time. I knew I had no intentions of stop using drugs in the near future so for the next two years I stopped taking insulin. It is no wonder I am experiencing all the different health problems I am dealing with today. I had stopped bathing and washing myself because I was spending all of my money on drugs. I had nothing left over to pay for the gas and electric, water and phone bills. So eventually they were turned off. I didn't mind so much that the phone and electricity being turned off. I was playing games with the gas and electric company. They would send someone over to turn off the electricity but I had learned how to turn it back on. Eventually, they removed the meter from the side of the house. The thing that really hit me hard was the turning off of the water. I need to say at this time there was an older couple that was living downstairs and had been living there ever since my father bought the house. They stayed there as long as they could take all the running in and out of the house of various people all times of the day and night and eventually they moved. Shortly after they moved I heard that the lady died from a heart attack and thereafter her husband died. I have always blamed myself for their deaths and was never able to contact their sons and tell them how sorry I was for my behavior. So when they moved I had an empty apartment downstairs. When the water was completely turned off in the upstairs apartment where I lived and I couldn't flush the toilet after having bowl movements I started using the bathroom downstairs and eventually that one got filled up. You can imagine the smell that was circulating in the whole house but at this point in my life I didn't care. All I cared about was using and chasing prostitutes.

I had also met this other guy who sold drugs and was the main supplier of this crack house in town. I would go with him to the house when he went to deliver his product and collect his money. After a period of time I became a regular fixture at that house. Before I knew it I had allowed myself to let some of the girls live at my house because they had no where to go. I had no knowledge of it but my house was becoming rapidly a crack and house of prostitution. Men who would pick women up and needed somewhere to take them would wind up at my house and by supplying me with a certain amount of drugs they could rent a room from me. So not only was I getting drugs whenever I wanted but women were coming along with the package. It became a point of not if I was going to get high but when I was going to get high. Still I was in big denial of my problem. I convinced myself that since I had somewhere to sleep and had steady income I wasn't as bad as those people in the streets were. Constantly staying high helped me stop thinking about the fact that my whole family was gone and why was God treating me like this.

In terms of deterioration and degradation of others and myself I was about to reach an all time high. In matter of fact how could I care about other people when it was obvious that I didn't care about myself. I would get up early in the morning and go to the local supermarket before people came around and go through the garbage looking for something or anything to eat. Since the electricity was turned off I would buy candles to heat the food I found in garbage cans to eat. I would go over to my aunt's house and eat the food that she had put aside for their cat. I remember one instance when my aunt asked me to paint her kitchen for her and what did I want for doing it for her. I told her to just feed me.

The house my mother left me was one of the nicest houses in the area we lived in. Before my mother got sick and died she spent many hours outside with her flowers, her vegetable garden and having the house look as good on the outside as it did in the inside. Inside the house there were very nice, expensive furniture that took my parents a while to accumulate. In the basement I had invested around $20,000 into my deejay system. I had arrived at a time where I was willing to sell or do anything to continue using. It sounds like an old cliché but anything that wasn't nail down had to go. In a very short period of time a house that was fully decorated became basically a very empty house. I didn't even care what the neighbor's thought when they saw things coming out of the house and nothing coming in. When there was nothing else to sell in the house then I started looking for things in the garage to sell. Things such as equipment to blow the leaves in the fall, to remove the snow in the winter and gardening tools my mother used in her garden. When I ran out of things outside to sell then I started renting my van out to drug dealers for drugs. Then I would have such a hard time getting my van back that eventually I gave up and never tried to get my van back. Then days would go by in the winter when I would be walking in the snow and would see someone drive by in my van.

I had been raised to respect women and under no circumstance to put my hands on females. The girl that was living with me I found myself constantly hitting her and kicking her in her pregnant stomach. I wouldn't touch her face because she needed to keep her looks in order to make money out there in the streets. I remember when I found out she was illiterate that I decided to use her issues of low self-esteem for my benefit. I remember I had taken her one day for a job at a local supermarket and when filling out the application under the section that deals with your sex she checked both. When I questioned her about it she responded by saying she has sex with both. It was at this time I realized that she was illiterate. She knew I could read and numerous times she asked me to teach her to read and my self centerness told me if she learn how to read that will lead to other things that will lead her not having to depend on me. Many days she would make me mad and I wouldn't let her in the house. I would look out at the window and see her sitting on the curb outside the house eating a sandwich and crying. The drugs had made me so hard and cruel I didn't care what I did to people or how much I hurt them. All I cared about was getting what I wanted, when I wanted it. I had become so vindictive that when she couldn't do anything sexually because of her health I would go out and find someone I knew she didn't like and bring her back to the house and let her see me with the other prostitute. When I thought that I couldn't sink any lower I continued to amaze myself. One of the girls that was working in that house of prostitution was a white girl that I had convinced to live and work out of my house. I eventually had around five different women living and working out of my house. I thought I had the perfect situation going for me. They would go out and get their johns and bring them back to the house. They would buy their drugs from me and in return they would give me a certain amount of drugs for using the house. This business finally turned into a friendship and I found myself caring for the safety of these women. I would walk them at night down to the boulevard to make sure nothing happened to them and that nobody tried to take advantage of them. I had convinced myself that I was being of service to them and that staying with me was the best thing for them. I had convinced myself that I was such a nice guy that one of the girls that was bringing in so much money and drugs I told her to take a week off and go visit with her son. Now where could she find someone like me that would do that for her?

One time this white girl had run into some money and she went and got a room in another town and called me and asked me to bring her some drugs. I arrived at her room and ended up staying there for about a week. I would only go out to get food and more drugs. Unknowing to us the neighbors next to us suspected something illegal was going on and they called the police department who in turn got in touch with their local narcotics task force. One night the task force came over and knocked on the door and busted in. The next thing I knew I had guns upside my head. I was arrested and taken down to the local police headquarters. Since the room and everything was registered in the girls name they released me because the person I had become put all the blame on her. They did everything they could think of to get me to reveal the name of the person I was getting my drugs from. She had told them that I had a friend who was a big time dealer in the area, but I wouldn't give up his name. In matter of fact when I was released the first thing I did was call him and tell him what happened and to be careful and not to come around my house for a while. What a true friend I believed I was to him. So I went home and continued living life as I was. I left that girl in jail to fend for herself and get out the best way she could. I never heard from her or about her again until I had to go to court many months later.

At this time I had this couple living in my house. They weren't paying me any money for rent. The guy was another drug dealer and that was how they were paying me rent. At first they seemed to be a loving, caring couple but later I realized they were fighting all the time, and I mean physical fighting. One evening they were at it again physical fighting. Another guy who happened to be in the house at this particular time and myself went to break it up and pull them apart. I need to say that at this time the men had a habit of sticking knives in the back of their pants with the blade exposed. The other guy had grabbed the women and I grabbed the man. Since I was bigger and stronger than he was I was pulling him backwards towards myself. The knife went in me twice. I was bleeding very badly and as I lay in the bed the woman did everything she could to stop the bleeding. I was in a lot of pain and the drug dealer would give me bottles for the pain. I noticed that every time I mentioned going to the hospital he would give me more bottles. It wasn't until later I found out that his fear was if I went to the hospital that the doctors were obligated to contact the police and unknown to me he had some warrants out for him. For about a week I just laid in the bed unable to do anything. I remember I had this woman staying there with me. I had been wanting to get with her for quite a while. I can recall us laying in the bed undressed and I being unable to do anything because of the wounds and pain. I guess after a while she started to think that there must be something wrong with me when I had this fine lady laying next to me naked and being unable to do anything. People had to help me to the bathroom, fix my meals and bring them to me. I didn't care; because I was getting drugs whenever I wanted them. I told myself I had the perfect situation. Eventually, I reached the point where no matter how many drugs he gave me it wouldn't ease the pain and I called my cousin and had her call the ambulance to take me to the hospital.

When I arrived at the hospital I was rushed right into surgery. Parts of my intestines were sticking out. I remember it was the day of the Super Bowl football game which began around 5:00 PM. When I went into surgery it was a little before 11:00 AM. I came out of surgery and was back in my room around 4:30 PM. I was in a lot of pain and the only thing I could think about was what could I do to ease the pain. I called a friend of mine and he asked me if there was anything he could do for me. I told him to bring me something to get high with. When he arrived with the drugs I told him to watch the door while I go in the bathroom and get high. My addiction had gotten to the point where it had taken over complete control of my logical thought process.

I need to say that even at this time in my life I had some real true friends. When I arrived home from the hospital I had this one friend who every day when he got out of work would stop by to see if I needed anything before he went home to see his girlfriend and kids. I had sent word to that couple that when I came home from the hospital that they couldn't be there or I would notify the police. The girls who were living there took care of me until my strength was to the point where I could take care of myself. Even going through this I wasn't ready to stop using drugs. I was still using on a regular basis and it was continually having a negative effect on the way I looked at the world, looked at myself, and how I treated others and myself. As soon as I regained my strength I found myself going back to the same type of lifestyle that had landed me in the hospital. I was due to report to court at this time for that charge when I was involved in that drug raid and since I knew I had no money to pay the fines or to hire a lawyer I just ignored the notice. Therefore a warrant had been issued for my arrest. As I started to run the streets again some people jumped me, but luckily I noticed who they were. I went to the police department to press charges against them and once the officer heard my name he informed me that they had a warrant for arrest. I was transferred to the county where the charges were logged. I went to court and pleaded innocent and was assigned a public defender. I was given a court date some months in the future.

Unknowing to myself my using days were about to end. Another drug dealer that I was aquatinted with had given me a package to sell for him in another town. He gave me some for myself so I wouldn't have to mess with his stuff. I arrived in town and got myself a room in a local motel. After smoking the stuff that he gave me for myself I started smoking the stuff he wanted me to sell. In the morning I found myself in a dilemma. If I went back home with no product or money I would probably get beat up and I was tired of getting beat up. Then I came up with this brilliant idea, which at that time I did not know was going to change my life. Since I was a veteran I could go to the local veteran hospital and go into the rehab for thirty days and then after that come home. My original intention was to convince the people that I owed the money and drugs to that since they hadn't heard from or seen me in a month that I had went to jail and since they hadn't been arrested that I probably protected their identify.

I went to this organization in town to get help and they put me up in this welfare motel until they could arrange a screening for me in the VA hospital.

I had received a call from the organization that had put me up and told me they had arranged a day for my screening. They gave me money for transportation but I went down for the screening on the wrong day. So when I was down there they informed me that my screening was for the next day. They told me they could put me up in a homeless shelter for the night, but I really fought that idea. I told the organization that was helping me that I wanted them to pay to bring me home and send me back the next day. They let me know that was not going to happen. They informed me if I wanted their help that I had to accept the help on their terms. Forced into a corner I had no other alternative but to spend the night at the homeless shelter. I found myself thinking how could I have arrived at this point in my life. My parents left me their house, money to live on, transportation to get around in and now I am forced to live in a homeless shelter. When I arrived at the shelter they gave me a mattress and then told me I would have to find somewhere to lay my mattress. I remember looking for a spot to place my mattress and seeing all the roaches and bugs running around on the floor. I have never been in a situation like that before. The next morning I got up and went for my screening. They told me I had been accepted and was giving me transportation money to go home and I had to wait for them to call me when they had a bed open up for me. I went home and the organization that was helping me out put me up back in the welfare motel until I received my phone call to report. While I was at home waiting on the call I was informed that they wanted me to report to their office every day and attend these twelve step meetings. I had to have these papers signed to prove that I was attending the meetings. During this period of time I was hiding out in my room because I couldn't take a chance of the people that had given me that package to sell for them to find me. Eventually, I received my call to report to the rehab because they had a bed open up for me.

AND YOU THOUGHT YOU COULDN'T CHANGE

PART 2

THE BEGINNING OF THE RISE BACK INTO REALITY

When I arrived at the rehab I need to say that I already had my mind made up about the reason why I was there and what I was going to do once I was there. I was only there for the thirty days and then head back to what I believed was the fun life. I need to point out also that most of my life I have been overweight and sported an Afro style haircut. Because of my drug usage and the lack of attention I had paid to my physical being I was weighing a little over 160 pounds. For the first time in years I had to have myself physically checked out and I found myself taking various medications for my health. I can't explain the reason why or when it happened but at some point down there I started listening to what the counselors were saying to me. The one thing that I remember that really had an impression on me was when one of the counselors was giving his definition of what a bottom was. He said that, "you had reached your bottom when the pain of what you were doing becomes greater than the pain of what you are running away from". Immediately I could identify with that. The pain of what I was doing was the constant drug use and the pain of what I was running away from was the thoughts of my whole immediate family being deceased and my being responsible for my mother and brother's death. I was being given a lot of things to think about and many nights after my counseling sessions I would lay in my bed thinking about the things that I had been discussing. Things such as being asked if I ever stole from my parents. Thinking that dealt in financial matters and my answer would always be no. Then they would discuss about how I stole from their piece of mind and rest when I was out there at night doing whatever and they were at home not knowing whether I was alive or dead. When discussing how I used drugs to have sex with women in relations to rape and being told that rape is not just a physical act. Being told that rape is anytime you hold something over someone's head and use that knowing they have no will power of their own to say no. Then I would be asked how would I feel if someone did that to a female relative of mine. My answer would be I wouldn't like it and then being told then what gives you the right to do that to other peoples relatives. I guess maybe God needs to get you alone by yourself where he can work on you. I was finally forced to look at my life, the opportunities I had and threw away, where my life was headed if I didn't make some definite changes in my life. For the first time in my life I was forced to talk about a lot of things that I chose to keep hidden inside of me. I think one of the major things that helped turn me around was the fact that I wouldn't listen to anyone telling me what I should do if they hadn't walked a mile in my shoes. Then I found out that a lot of the counselors down there were actually people who had lived the lifestyle I was living and I couldn't pull anything over on them. I realized that anything I would come up with that I thought was smart and slick they had already thought of and done. So for the first time in my life I found myself actually listening. When I was about to finish with that program it was suggested to me that I needed long-term treatment and now I was willing to listen and try whatever they recommended to me. It made a lot of sense to me when they said, "you can try and do things our way for a few months and then after that time if you do not like it you can go back to doing things your way and have your misery refunded". For the first time in years I was feeling good about myself. I had been drug free for thirty days. They told me they would contact this other long-term veterans program near where I lived and put my name on the list for a bed. I would have to go home and wait for the call that they had a bed for me. I contacted the organization that had helped me before and they said they were willing to put me back up in the motel until it was time to go to the other rehab, but I would have to follow their instructions. I remember calling my aunt to come and get me. When my aunt arrived there she did not know who I was because I had put some weight on. I had begun to shave my head and keep it shaved even today because I did not want anything to remind me of what I looked like when I went through all those years of using.

  I arrived back at home and found myself following their instructions. I would take any suggestions that they would give me. I found myself going back to church. They told me I needed to continue attending these twelve step meetings and I found myself going to those meetings two or three times a day. They told me the most important thing was to stay away from other people that I knew who were still active in that lifestyle and I followed that suggestion to. When I would go to these twelve step meetings I would for the first time rather than just sitting in the back and being quiet I found myself sitting up front and talking about myself, my feelings, the things I was going through and generally asking for help. I believe it was at this point in time that I had made the decision that I never wanted to go back to that lifestyle. That was April 5, 1995 and thanks to God and my friends I have never returned to that lifestyle. Eventually, I received my phone call that they had a bed for me and they needed me to come the next day. I reported the next day and my life has never been the same ever since.

    I arrived there and would stay there for the next eight months. I have always been one of those people who thought that only weak people go to other people for counseling because they are not strong enough to handle and deal with their own problems. One of the first things they told me that they felt I needed to do was to learn how to deal with grief and to do that they wanted me to see this counselor twice a week. Even though I didn't believe in it I was willing to try anything. I need to say that even today if I am going through something I will sometimes call that same counselor and ask her if she has some time to discuss something with me.

    I recall one of the counselors there had told me that she did not think I would make it due to my attitude when I first arrived there. A lot of times my motivation comes when people tell me that I can't do something or achieve a goal that I set my sights on. At nighttime I would sign the list to go on the van that was taking people to various twelve-step meetings. When I attended all the various classes we were required to during the daytime I found myself actually listening to what the counselors were talking about. After being there for about a month the second phase of the program went into effect. We had to find employment and they kept track of the money we were making and how we were spending it. The purpose was to make sure at the end of our time there we had enough money to get an apartment and begin a new life. When most of the veterans would go home on the weekends I would stay there. One thing I found it amazing was that this rehab was for homeless veterans but every weekend the veterans had somewhere to go. It was important to me to save as much money as I could to get my apartment when I left there. When at the end of the eight months it was time to discharge me it was around Christmas time. I asked the staff if it would be all right if I stayed there until after the New Year. They told me that since I had been a model client and did not cause any problems they did not see any problems with letting me stay there until after the New Year. I had found an apartment in my hometown and they had told me that they did not recommend that I go back there and that I should find housing in another town where I did not know anyone. To me that wasn't a viable solution because I truly believed that if I was going to use I would use and it really didn't matter where I was. So after New Years in the year 1996 I moved into my apartment.

I was on a journey to begin a new life. I was quite fortunate because I had saved quite a bit of money while I was at the rehab. I was still receiving money from my mother's trust each month and had arranged for that money to be automatically deposited into a bank account for me. When I first arrived home I was worried about having a lot of cash on my person so I had my aunt handle my money for me until I felt comfortable enough to handle my money on my own. At this time I didn't have transportation of my own so I was catching buses or trains to attend these twelve step meetings at night. I found myself actually listening to what they were saying and how they were staying away from drugs and dealing with life's events on life's basis.

I had started going back to church. I remember talking with my aunt and she told me that I had proved to her the power of prayer. She told me she would pray for me over and over again without any success. When she finally gave up and left it in God's hand the next thing she knew I was in rehab. I remember when I first arrived home my friend who owned the local bar in town had asked me if I wanted to come back and deejay for her. I thanked her for the offer but told her I just couldn't be in an environment where alcohol and drugs were present. Any time she was having problems with her deejay system I would come in and take a look at it and fix it for her, but that was the extent of my coming around there. When I first got my apartment the only thing I had in it was a mattress that was given to me by the housing people at the rehab. Because I didn't have a television or radio in it there was a lot of silence there and I had to learn to be comfortable with just being by myself without having outside elements to validate my existence. People were helping me assemble things for my apartment piece by piece. I had went to the local Social Services Department and applied for welfare and foodstamps and was approved. For the first time in my life I was taking care of myself and not depending on other people to take care of me. I was taking medicine regularly for my diabetes and high blood pressure.

Part of my getting welfare and food stamps was I had to go and register for work with the local Unemployment office. When I went there I was directed to go and talk wit the local veteran's representative. Upon talking with the representative he suggested that I go up to the local community college and talk with this individual who deals with non-traditional students concerning returning back to school. I need to say that when I went to talk with the representative I had no intention of returning to school. This was the year 1996 and I had left high school in the year 1970, but I also knew that I had to follow through with any recommendations the Unemployment office made if I wanted to continue to collect my welfare and food stamps. After talking with the school counselor I left there thinking that maybe I could do that, but I was not ready to go to school and have to sit in classes with kids young enough to be my own kids. When I came back and met with the veteran's representative I was coming up with all these various excuses why I couldn't follow through and every excuse I came up with he would come up with a reason how I could. I told him I didn't have any money to go to school with and he told me they had something called a veteran's waiver where the school would waive my first year's tuition because I was a veteran. Then when I told him I didn't have any transportation to get to college he gave me a schedule book of the local shuttle bus that goes back and forth to the college. When I told him I had been out of school for over twenty years and was probably way behind all the other students he told me they had remedial courses for non-traditional students who are returning back to school. So after running out of excuses I register to start college in the spring of 1997. They even had me go to financial aid and file for a job on campus and was given a job at the counseling department which I would hold the whole time I was attending Raritan Valley Community College.

When I first began attending Raritan Valley Community College I had decided that I wanted to do something that I never did before when I was in school and that was to become involve in after class activities. I had asked someone I knew where did all the pretty girls hang out and the answer was in the Orguello Latino Club. So I went about to find out where they had their meeting and when I found out I attended their next meeting. I went to the meeting and asked them if I need to speak Spanish in order to join their club and their response was no. So I joined the club. I do not believe they thought I was serious but after I continue to come to the meetings week after week they began to realize that I was serious. Another reason I joined was to start to get some diversity in my life. In the fall of 1998 when the club started up they asked me if I would like to be their representative at the student government meetings, and I agreed to. As I started becoming involved with the student government I became a good friend with the president of student government. I need to say that the president of student government was a white girl and one year knowing my history of my entire family being deceased her family had me over for a Thanksgiving dinner so I wouldn't have to spend it alone. The same time they had this program on campus called the Mentoring Program. This was a program designed for minorities to have staff or administrative people to act as role models. I think the person I chose, as my mentor was the best decision I had made next to stop using drugs and going back to school. That person was the college's president. In the fall of that semester there was a meeting at Rider University where some students were trying to organize the students all over the state to address student issues. The people that were suppose to go with our student government president bailed out at the last minute and she came to me and worried me about going to the meeting until I finally gave in. This was the third best decision I had made since stop using drugs and asking the college president to be my mentor. The reason why that was the third best decision I made was that by going to this meeting I met Dr. John Pace of Essex County College and members of the New Jersey Student County College Coalition.

NEW JERSEY STUDENT COUNTY COLLEGE COALITION

When I returned to Raritan Valley Community College from the meeting at Rider University I became more involved with the student government along with the New Jersey Student Community College Coalition. During this semester the secretary of the student government resigned and my friend who was president of student government told me that she wanted to recommend me for secretary. After some thought and discussion with my mentor I agreed to take the secretary position. In the beginning of the spring semester the vice president and treasurer of student government did not return so my friend asked me to step up and take the vice president position. I agreed to. At this time the president was pregnant and eventually before the semester was over she would resign and I was asked to step up and be president. At this time I was doing the president, vice president and treasurer positions. I was also getting more involved with the New Jersey Student Community College Coalition. I would make some speeches before the New Jersey Commission of Higher Education.

When I first started at Raritan my major was Human Services. Because I had been out of school for so many years I was enrolled in a number of remedial courses. When I was in high school I never tried to succeed in my classes because I would see my brother bring home C's and D's and my parents would not say that much to him. When I brought home the same type of grades in an effort to emulate my brother they would go off on me. Then when I would improve my grades I would get no kind of acclamation like my brother would get and he wasn't bringing home good grades. At Raritan College I would end up being an honor student getting all A's and B's. I realized that the teachers there were not my enemy and were there to help me. I learned to swallow my pride and ask other students who were young enough to be my own kids to help me. The ironic thing is I would eventually tutor the same kids that I would go to for help. Towards the end of this semester I was in English class taking a final exam and had my first seizure. I was told that I had become violent and was unconscious for about half an hour. I was in the hospital for about a month taking all kinds of test and then released. I was told I would be able to return in the fall.

Towards the end of the semester the student government advisor to student government approached me about running for president for the following school year. I agreed to do so. At the same time the advisor to the New Jersey Student Community College Coalition approached me about running for statewide president of their organization. I discussed this with my mentor and he advised me to run for statewide president. He told me that I could do more for the students as statewide president. He remarked that I had nothing else to gain by serving as president of student government for another year. So I withdrew from the election for president of student government. The funny thing was that my opponent barely won and he was running unopposed. Even though I had resigned people were voting for me on absentee ballots. At the end of the spring semester when we had the student government awards ceremony I was presented with the award for student leadership and citizenship. I was also inducted into the Who's Who Among Students in American Junior Colleges. I won the election for statewide president of the New Jersey Student Community College Coalition. I didn't take the summer off. I took some courses during the summer at Raritan. Also, during the spring semester I had a talk with my mentor and he told me if I plan to have a future or hold political office I should give an interview and talk about my past. By discussing my past first people would not be able to use my past against me and that I could hold the interview at the college. So I contacted the local paper and they came to the college to do the interview.

When the fall semester began I found myself very busy. Before the first day of class the president and college had a surprise for me. Usually, before classes start the college has something called All College Day where all the staff and administrative personnel comes to the college to discuss what they plan to achieve in the coming school year. Students are never invited to attend these meetings. I was invited. When I arrive the president presented me a copy of the article that had been written about me in the spring and the College had it framed. As statewide president we had formed chapters of the organization at various community colleges. Along with our advisor, some of the executive members of the New Jersey Student Community College Coalition were traveling around the state giving presentations of the organization and how we could be of service to them. At the same time I was going to the Commission of Higher Education meetings in Trenton every month and maintaining my A average in my studies. We had begun to lobby for this bill that would allow the student representatives who sit on the Commission of Higher Education the right to vote. We also were involved with this bill that allow tuition aid grant for part time students. At the same time I was still attending my twelve step meetings and having regular attendance in church. I had enrolled in a program called Operation Bluepoint, which was sponsored by the local United Way. This program was designed to teach individuals the necessary skills to participate on local Board of Directors committees of non-profit organizations. After completing this program I joined the Board of Directors of the Somerset Treatment Services, where I am still an active member. Also, during this time other members of the executive committee and myself met with various legislators around the state and also with the Governor twice. At the various community colleges chapters we were organizing voter registration drives. There was one incident that happened to me that I remember with quite a bit of fondness. I had put in to take this honors writing course at the College and my English professor had sent in her letter of recommendation. When the professor in charge of the class received my request she turned it down stating that she just didn't think I qualify for the course. I think my English professor took it harder than I did. I think she took it personally, like her recommendation was not good enough for this one professor. Anyway, later on when the professor found out who I was and that I was speaking before the state legislature on a regular basis her attitude towards me changed. One day she saw me in school and asked me who wrote my testimonies when I would speak before the legislature and when I responded that I write all of my own testimonies she informed me that maybe she had made a mistake. Then she asked me if I still wanted to take her class and I told her no. I told her if I am good enough to write my own testimonies and speak before the State Legislator, Governor and Commission of Higher Education meetings that I really do not need her course. I don't think she took that to well.

  This same schedule and pace of activities continued into the spring semester. I was approaching my last semester at Raritan before it was time for me to graduate. As I was approaching graduation time and considering transferring to a four-year institution I ran into some problems with transferring credits. I wanted to enter the social work program at a nearby university and they told me they would not accept my social work credits because the professor who taught the course had a Masters Degree in Sociology and not Social Work. At this point this was another issue for me to get involved in. I did a lot of research concerning this issue and started speaking on the issue when I went to the Commission of Higher Education meetings. Eventually the state of New Jersey would address this issue. Then when I went to the university I wanted to transfer to and I went to the political science department and they informed me they would accept all of my credits. I remember talking with my mentor about it and he told me he felt I was heading in that direction but he didn't say anything to me because it needed to be my decision. The university accepted me to begin the fall semester as a junior. During the commencement ceremonies the Governor was the guest speaker and she made a few references towards me. Even though my entire family is deceased I think they would have been proud of the man I was becoming and there would be a lot more changes to be witnessed in that process.

During the summer the executive branch of the organization was having meetings and making our strategic plans for the upcoming school year. One of the major things we discussed was the changing of our name from the New Jersey Student Community College Coalition to the New Jersey Student College Coalition, or simply SC^2. After doing some research we had found out that we were the only active student group in the state that was out there defending the rights of college students in higher education and that it shouldn't matter whether you are in a community college, technical college or four year university. So we decided to change our name to reflect that idea and then we had to go through our constitution to also reflect that concept. It was also during this summer that we were contacted by a local television station to do a 90 second ad on the issue of Tuition Aid Grant for part time students that we were lobbying for.

With every thing that was going on with me I was still maintaining all A's and B's in my classes. I was taking classes also during this summer. I was still going to my twelve step meetings at night because I knew that I had to stay clean and not use because if I started using again then everything that I had worked so hard to accomplish would be gone with one light of the pipe.

This summer I was able to do something that I hadn't been able to do since my mother died and that was to visit the grave site where my brother, father, and mother was buried. There is one spot left there and that is for me. It was the first time that I felt worthy and deserving to go there. I knew for so long I wasn't living my life in accordance to the morals and values they tried to implant in me as a young child. For the first time in a long time I was starting to feel good about myself. I was starting to be able to look at myself in the mirror and not wonder who in the world this person was and how I got myself into this position. I was starting to believe what my mentor at Raritan Valley use to tell me. He would say that some people are born to be followers and some are leaders and that I was a leader. I had been a follower all my life and believed that is what I was destined to be. I had been taking care of myself for a while now. I had my own apartment, had furnished it completely, was cooking my own meals, and washing my own clothes. The highlight of this summer was when one of the local newspapers contacted me and told me they wanted to do an article on me and wanted to do it at my apartment. So the night of the interview they came over and set up on my porch with all the different lights and cameras. My neighbors were walking by and stopping and wondering what was going on. When they read the article in the paper people were stopping by and telling me how proud they were of me. Some people that had bought drugs from me in the past had stopped by and told me that they hope some day they could do the same thing as I had done. You can't imagine how good that made me feel inside. I was starting to feel worthwhile, that I was no longer a menace to society and that I had started to gain people's respect.

So the fall semester started and I was ready for this new adventure. Studying at a university was a lot different than at a community college but I felt I was up for the challenge. I was focused on keeping my grade average up as an honor student. Also, as president of the New Jersey Student College Coalition the group was really involved into getting this bill that would allow the student representatives who sit on the Commission of Higher Education the right to vote passed by the legislature. Since my major was political science I knew that if we didn't push to have the bill pass in the legislature by the first couple of weeks in January we would have to start the process all over again. So when we had our yearly statewide conference one of the things on the agenda was to get the point across that it was very important that we get the bill voted on by the legislature before the new legislature is sworn in on January. Students were calling and writing their legislators and imploring them to get the Speaker of the Assembly to post the bill. Matter of fact at the conference one of the speakers was the Chairman of the Assembly Education Committee and he was telling us how he was on our side and would do whatever he could from his end to get the bill posted. Also, at the conference I was voted in as statewide president for another year. At the university the political science department believed that part of learning about politics is not just lecturing to the students but actually going to functions and activities where the various legislators would be. They believed that this approach would give the students an opportunity to interact with the state politicians. They arranged all kind of trips for us. I took part in various functions such as a retreat for the College Leadership of New Jersey, Campaign 2000 in Washington, DC and every November all the mayors in the state would meet down in Atlantic City. When I was down at the conference in Atlantic City I happened to run into the Speaker of the Assembly and was able to speak to him for a few minutes about posting the bill. After giving him my reasons why I felt he should post the bill he asked me if I really thought it was a good bill. I replied in the affirmative and he responded saying he would consider it when he went back to his office. A few days after the conference was over I had received a letter from his office stating that he was going to post the bill and have the legislature vote on it and requested my appearance on the date of the vote. I was there on the date of the vote and it passed 72-0. The next thing really took me by surprise. The Speaker of the Assembly asked me to stand up and be recognized me in front of the whole state legislature for the work that the New Jersey Student College Coalition and myself had done to get the bill voted on.

In the past when the group met with the Governor she told us that if the bill reached her desk s he would sign it into law. So we knew that since the bill had been sent to her desk that it would be signed into law. After the bill was signed into law the Governor arranged for the group to come in for a photo shot and she personally signed copies of the bill for members of the group. That was one of the highlights of the group's achievements.

The spring semester was basically a repeat of the other semesters. I was working hard on my classes to maintain my honor grade status. I was still making my meetings at night at the twelve-step fellowship and going ahead with other issues for the group to get involved in. Now that we were being taken seriously by the powers to be that were making the major political decisions in the state, the next issue we tackled was Tuition Aid Grant for part time students. The group was continually being represented at the Commission of Higher Education monthly meetings, and have different members speak. During this time the political science department at the university had arranged for some of their students to attend the Republican and Democratic National Convention. I attended the Republican National Convention in Philadelphia, Pennsylvania. That was a learning experience. They had all the major political players in the party from around the country there to nominate George Bush for President. In the morning we would attend lectures and classes and the afternoon we would go to the Convention Hall. I was real excited when returning from the convention and then received an invitation to attend a national conference of student leaders in Minnesota. I attended with two other members of the group. When first contacted about attending I asked them why was I asked. I was told that the committee in charge of invitations had contacted some people in New Jersey that I didn't know. They had said that I was probably the most influential student in the state. When hearing that I felt so good inside. At the same time I was still attending the monthly meetings of the Commission of Higher Education.

Around the same time I was working on planning another statewide conference. Because of my academic status I was contacted by the university and asked if I would like to spend my last semester studying in London, England. I was ecstatic with the opportunity that was being presented to me. It didn't take my any time to decide that I was going to go to England. At our statewide conference I announced that my tenure as president for two years was about to come to an end and that they need to start looking for someone to step up and take my place. At the conference I was awarded a plaque by the group for the work I had done for two years as their statewide president. Usually, I am not short of words but at this time I found myself speechless. The two years that I was president I was constantly being called for interviews and posing questions to me concerning the direction the group was going and the new issues we were working on, but now I was speechless. That summer I spent a great deal of time helping the group get ready for the transition of the new administrative body, also I had to get ready for my trip to England the following spring.

That fall I spent a lot of time getting things ready before I left the United States to go and study in England. I had to get my visa and select the type of program I would study when I arrived in England. Even though at this time they had a new statewide president for the group I was still active in the group. I would take part in voter registration drives. The director of the New Jersey Transfer Program at a local community college also contacted me. This was a program designed and supported and financed by the state to deal with the issue of transferring college credits from one institution to another. They were starting a newsletter and wanted me to write an article for them because I was the first one to bring this problem to the attention of the state a few years earlier when I spoke before the Commission of Higher Education. I agreed and wrote the article for them.

As I was preparing to leave for England I was treated in a way that was completely new to me. The members of my group had given me a going away party. One of the members of my twelve step meetings that I attend at night gave me a going away party in this club in New York and members had driven from New Jersey to help give me a send off. Nobody had ever did anything like that for me. For the first time in my life I was genuinely starting to feel that people liked me for the person I had become and not what they felt they could get from me. Many of the legislators that I had developed a friendship at the state capitol were wishing me success in my new adventure abroad. What made it even more special to me was the fact that I didn't keep my past secret so all these people knew about my past and still liked me anyway. A few weeks before I was to leave one of my professors from the political science department contacted me and let me know that he had arranged for some of the students to attend the Presidential Inauguration in Washington, DC. He was asking me if I wanted to attend. What a dilemma. It was around the same time I was to be leaving for England. After doing much thinking about it and discussing it with some of my friends I made the decision to forgo the Inauguration and go to England. Even today I think I made the right decision.

ENGLAND

My trip to England was similar and also different at the same time to the previous times I had been outside of the United States. It was the third time in my life that I had been outside of the country. A year earlier after fall recess I went to Can Cun, Mexico for a week. What was similar was I slept all the way over to England and Thailand. The thing that was different was that when I went to Thailand I was still using and when I went to England I had been clean for about six years. The study abroad program director had already arranged for me to stay with an English family. Before I went to Thailand I had an idea of what to expect because I had spoken with some people that had been over there already but I had nothing to prepare myself for what I was about to experience.

When I first arrived in England I noticed a few things right off the bat that was different than things in the United States. One of the differences was that in the cars the steering wheel was on the right side of the car rather than on the left like in the United States. Also, the streets were a lot smaller. Over there it seemed like the cars had the right of way instead of the pedestrian so you had to be real careful about crossing the streets. The cars were driven on the opposite side of the road. The house that I was staying at had another student from Spain and I was able to talk to him for awhile. One of the first things I had to learn to understand was their currency and how to turn American money into pounds. Another difference was the supermarkets are a lot different than in the United States. Many of the foods that I eat at home they did not have in England. So I had to adjust my diet and eating habits to the food they had over there. Also, when doing grocery shopping you had to do your own bagging of groceries. Another big difference was in their restaurants. Unlike in the

United States, when you go into a restaurant you pay first and then are seated and then they bring you your meal. You do not have to remove your empty trays after you finish eating the waiters do that. There is no tipping of the waiters because their fee is included as part of the bill. Every corner there seems to be a pub. There is a lot more churches in England than in the United States. Their malls though are like the ones we have in the states, and using the subways and trains in New York had trained me to use the subways and trains system in England.

I lived in walking distance of the university and down town area so I did not have to depend on public transportation. I have seen pictures of double decker buses, but had never rode in one until I went to England. I rode on them once and that was it for me because I felt very uncomfortable. I was constantly thinking that the bus at some point in time would turn over. Our professors taught completely different than the one's back home. It was mostly lectures and you really did not have to buy any textbooks. My classes meet once a week for each particular subject rather than two or three times a week like in the United States. When I first started school there I went to the university library and set up an e-mail account so I could keep in touch with everyone back home. During orientation I noticed that many of my classmates were from various countries all over the world. When I first arrived in England I found out where they had some twelve-step meetings and made arrangements to attend them while I was there. During orientation I made friends with a guy from Morehouse College in Atlanta, Georgia and we would eventually spend a lot of time together.

I went exploring my immediate surroundings and found a local post office, laundry mat and supermarket. What I really liked about being in England was how visitor friendly the people were. They were never too busy to stop and help out a stranger. What I really liked was there was never any dogs running around loose so walking home at night you really could feel at ease and comfortable. When people would take their dogs out for a walk they had them on a leash and always carried a bag with them to pick up any mess their dog might happen to do. They took real care into keeping their gardens looking nice and neat. It reminded me of all the hard work my mother use to put into keeping her gardens nice and presentable and then after she died how I let the garden died just like my mother had died. It looked so much different than some of the communities here in the United States. When I went through orientation after I first arrived in England I found out that I was able to work there part time. So I went through their process of obtaining their version of a social security card and then I was able to get myself a part time job on campus. This job helped me get past many of the days when I had no class and had nothing to do with myself. The president of the community college that I had graduated from who was mentor had transferred to another college in Texas where he was the president of. We kept in touch with each other by way of the e-mail system. When I first arrived in England he had sent me some money to pay my rent in advance so I would be able to really enjoy this opportunity and not to worry about financial issues. Since I was spending so much time in my room I had purchased myself a television and started watching British soap operas and really enjoyed them. Even today when I am skimming through the channels to find something to watch and something from England is on I will watch it. To me their sitcoms were more realistic than the ones we have in the United States because they dealt with real life situations. It rained quite often over in England and I never took into consideration that since England was an island surrounded by water that at night it would get quite chilly. Another thing that really impressed me was how openly the British would show how they felt about one another. The holding of hands was not a rare occasion like back home. I had found out where the local twelve step fellowship meetings were at where I lived and members would pick my up and bring me home from the meeting. Usually after the meeting was over they would go to a diner and would always invite me to attend. This was rarely done to me in the United States.

Another difference that I noticed in England that I kind of liked was the fact that when you are buying something you pay no additional taxes. I had signed up for classes that I had already taken in the United States. It was curious to me how the English professors were going to teach courses dealing with politics and solutions to the problems we have here in the United States when they couldn't solve their own problems. When I first arrived in England they were having this big controversy concerning the presidential election in the United States and the counting of votes down in Florida and people in England were asking me questions because they didn't understand it. I found it amazing because people in the United States who claimed to be political analysis didn't understand it. I noticed the work in the classes were more complexed. There is more reading assignments in my classes. I made an appointment with the health clinic on campus and was able to get my regular medication for my diabetes. Another difference I noticed in England in comparison to the United States was that the police did not carry guns. I couldn't understand how they were able to maintain peace and order without guns. Another difference is the delivery of the mail by their postal service. The mailman rode bicycles when delivering mail house to house. Another difference was the use of portable bathrooms all over the downtown area, which I wish they would implement in the United States. In their talk shows it is non-stop without the constant interruption of commercials. Also, I believe that the government controls the heat in the homes. The heat goes on and off at certain intervals and there is no instrument in the house for you to turn the heat up or down.

One of the classes that were mandatory for me to take dealt with British life and culture. I had to do a research paper dealing with that issue. After doing some research I decided to do my paper on Pam Am Flight #103 that exploded over Lockerbie, Scotland on December 21, 1998 killing all 259 people o board and another 11 on the ground. I did my paper from the perspective of the effect the trial had on the residents of Lockerbie. Even today I can not understand how two people can be tried for the same incident and one was found guilty and the other one innocent. I am starting to understand some of the terminology they used over there. For example, they use the word solictor, when referring to a lawyer. When I went searching for a part time job I found out in England that you have to have a bank account, because you are paid by direct deposit. In England their main sports are rugby and soccer. There is even a soccer field nearby where I stay. I am beginning to watch these activities and actually understand them. I was finding myself blending in with their culture. For some unknown reason I was starting to drink a lot of tea. In the house where I was living at I had for the first time in my life an opportunity to use a washer and dryer for the dishes. In one of my classes we were taught about the English educational system and I was amazed how completely different it is to the United States. It seems to me that in England they are more concerned about the students than in the United States. It is amazing how many cigarettes the British smoke. It seems like they are chain smokers. Because I do not smoke and smoke irritates me I had to select certain meetings to go to at nighttime that are non-smoking. You would be amazed with the quantity of people in England who use cellular phones. In the morning when the kids are downtown waiting for the bus to go to school it seems like all of them have cellular phones.

I was only there for about a month and I had volunteered to serve as an information assistant for the Open House they were having for new students who were considering attending the university. I was finding myself doing things I would never have done before. One such thing was having frequent conversations with my landlord concerning certain aspects of the British culture that I did not understand. Around this time I had received an exciting e-mail from my cousin from Atlanta, Georgia. She had told me that she had always wanted to visit England and now that I was there she was going to take a vacation and come over with her two sons. I remember going to the Ashmolean Library and our guide there showing us outside actual footprints of dinosaurs. I was also taking a lot of pictures to have a remembrance of my stay in England and the various places that I was fortunate enough to attend. While thinking about this there is one thing that I do regret. When I was in Thailand and had traveled to Cambodia, China and other points of interest in Southeast Asia I was so involved into my using that I never thought of taking pictures so I would be able to reflect years later of my stay over there. Many nights when I would attend my meetings I would think whether or not all this would have happened to me if I had continued using drugs. I think not__

Being a political science major I had found it quite interesting studying the British Parliament and their government as it contrast to the American government. I couldn't wait until we went on our field trip to Parliament. I have met some black females who attend the university and told me they do not drink but they enjoy the club scene and I should join them sometime. Personally, I chose to continue in the lifestyle I was living. That lifestyle consisted of going to the university for classes, check my e-mail or go to my job at the campus store and then going to meeting at night and spending the rest of the time in my room watching television. At this time I was still having these mood swings dealing with how I felt about myself and then I was asked to talk to some of the inmates at a maximum-security prison. That experience left me with a lot of gratitude, realizing that could have been me in the United States.

My cousin arrived with her two sons and we had a very enjoyable time. I took them for lunch at this Lebanese Restaurant near where I lived and then we got on the train and I took them to London. We walked past the Bath, the house of Parliament and the changing of the guard at Buckingham Palace. While my cousin was there I also noticed some behavior that was different than in the United States. It didn't bother me but my cousin was completely astonished by it. We say two women who obviously were involved in a relationship kissing and holding hands in public.

After my cousin left and I returned to class we went on a field trip to learn the history of the English Theater. In some of my classes I had two girls who attended the same university in the states that I was attending. We visited the Globe Theater where Shakespeare wrote and performed many of his plays. At nighttime I went to see an actual play in the English Theater by Oscar Wilde. The play was called "The Importance of Being Ernest." It was performed at the famous English Savoy Theater. I had never attended any plays in New York because I really did not think I would be interested in them. What a big mistake I had made. I really enjoyed this play, but then maybe the plays in England would be a lot different that the one's in the states. In one of my classes the professor did something that I found quite stimulating. The class was in Comparative Politics and we had a debate. One student was from Sweden, another one from Germany and myself. Three different students who came from different countries with different forms of government participated in this debate. The professor picked a subject and we had to make a statement concerning the question and defend it. What made it interesting was I had to pretend I was from Germany, the Swedish student had to pretend she was from the United States and the German girl had to pretend she was from Sweden. After the debate I spent the rest of the day in the hospital. I had gone to the health center on campus and they told me to go to the local hospital and have a complete checkup on my diabetes and my kidneys. As far as my health was concerned anything they told me to do I did because I did not want to take any chance of getting sick over there, with all my doctors who really know me and my medical records were back in the states.

As I traveled around England going to different twelve step meetings in various towns I was constantly being asked to come back and speak. One day I went to a meeting in Camdentown and after the meeting some of the members asked me if I would like to hang out with them and go to a fund-raiser in the area. I did and I can say that I really enjoyed myself. I was even afforded the opportunity to go up to one of the London Bobbies and ask for direction. I really got a kick out of that. During the time I was in England the farmers were having a big problem with Food and Mouth Disease, associated with the cattle, and whether or not Prime Minister Blair should postpone his reelection for Prime Minister until they dealt with this disease.

I was running out of the insulin that I use for my diabetes and hadn't received my shipment from the states. So I went to the health services on campus and they sent me to a chemist to get the equivalent of what I was taking. In one of my classes I had to do a presentation of "Green Parties" so I was spending a lot of time in the library and at home at night doing research. Also, around this time I went to the ATM machine to take some money out and couldn't remember my pin number. You have to understand that my account was from the bank in the states, so there was nothing the banks in England could do for me. Even though I had plenty of money in it I couldn't get anything out until I remembered my pin number. Once I remembered you could bet I wrote it down first thing.

Towards the middle of the semester our class went on a tour of Big Ben and the House of Parliament. We actually were inside the House of

Parliament where the British Cabinet meets and learned about how the Queen's position is more a title than a position. We saw the Queen's throne and crown. We also got an opportunity to rub the foot of the statute of Sir Winston Churchill. In another month we will be on a month's vacation. Most of the students were planning their trips to other countries. My friends from Kean University had asked me if I wanted to travel with them country jumping, but I knew there would be a lot of drinking and drugging so I turned down the offer. I already had made my plans previously for the spring break. The first week of our spring break I was planning on attending a convention of the twelve step fellowship meetings I attend at night. The week before the convention I was going to work at the campus store and then after the convention I was going to Paris, France for a week. One day I had a very interesting class. I did a presentation for my Urban American History class on riots, ghettos and civil rights. After my presentation many of my classmates were asking a lot of questions and I was able to give them actual first hand information that the professor was not able to give them. We were unable to visit Stonehenge because of the Food and Mouth Disease, so we went to visit the town of Bath and went on a tour of the Roman Baths. I had also received an invitation to appear on the Trisha talk show. This would be my second time being on a nationwide television show. Before I left for England I was on the Queen Latifa talk show in New York.

I had to do a presentation in one of my classes with two other British students. I really enjoyed working with them. I think we did a pretty good job on our presentation. Another difference I found out between England and America is at the train station you have to pay to use the restrooms. Around this time I had received a letter from Kean University stating that I had been nominated to be a member of Who's Who Among Students at American Universities and Colleges.

I was on a month's spring break and worked for a week until it was time for the convention. At first I didn't think I would like the convention because it was being held in a high school and not in an expensive hotel like I was use to back in the states. I was surprised though. I really enjoyed myself. I had people coming up to me telling me they had heard about me and asking me if I would come to the town where they lived and speak before I left for America. I met a couple from New Orleans that I became good friends with and we kept in touch with each other through the internet. Around this time I was noticing that I was having a hard time staying awake in the daytime. It won't be until I came back home to the states and was diagnosed with sleep apnea, that I will understood why I kept falling asleep. Around this time I went to a meeting in London and celebrated my six years clean. I went to this one meeting and this one lady gave me her six-year medallion since I was not able to get one from the meetings I go to in the states. There are no words to express the joy and gratitude I felt inside of me. Around this time I had also received a letter from one of my former supervisors at Kean. I knew when I returned home I would have my Bachelor's degree and was interested in going to graduate school. I knew graduate school would be expensive and I needed to find a way to apply to be a graduate assistant. Graduate assistants are able to have all their tuition waived by the university. Plus, I found myself in a dilemma because the deadline had already past. This letter from my former supervisor was asking me if I would like to be her graduate assistant. I couldn't believe it. Then I received a check from Kean for $1200. I couldn't believe how well God was blessing me.

After the convention was over I left to spend a week in Paris, France. I took the Eurostar train, which took only about five hours to get from London to Paris, France. Once I arrived in Paris it was like cultural shock to me. The hotel that I was staying in was only a few blocks from the train station. People talk about the homeless people in America and how depressing their situation is. People in the United States should see the homeless people in other countries before they start complaining. I had a hard time communicating and asking for directions when I arrived in Paris. I had always thought of English as a universal language and believed that everyone knew how to speak English. Boy, was I about to find out different. My first day there I decided just to stay in my room and rest. I had a television in my room, but all the language was in French. Imagine watching the Cosby's and all the dialogue is in French. On my second day there I decided to take the grand tour of Paris. Some of the places that I visited were the Opera House, Notre Dame Cathedral, Luxembourg (where Parliament meets), Saint Gerrmain, Museed Orsay and the Eiffel Towel. I need to say that over there my desire to use drugs had been lifted but I found myself in a real battle not to pick up prostitutes or go to live sex shows because I was so lonely over there. I was beginning to understand that all the material things I had been blessed to achieve meant nothing if you did not have someone to share these things with. I had to keep telling myself that I deserve better than that and if I had been brought this far then there probably is someone else out there waiting for me, if only I would be patient. At the same time when I went to see the Notre Dame Cathedral, I had a charcoal portrait of myself done by one of the artist down by the river and I also went inside the Notre Dame Cathedral and prayed.

I really did not like the people that I ran into in France. They are not tourist friendly. One of the differences I noticed between France and

England is that in France the police do carry guns. For the week I was in France I had to become use to the French currency. I had just started understanding the pound system on England and now I have to understand the frank system in France.

When I arrived back in England I had some letters from Kean University informing me that I had received quite a few awards and since I was out of the country I would be given them when I returned. For awhile I was disappointed because I would not be able to participate in the graduation ceremony, since the ceremony was in May and I would not be returning to the states until June. But I looked at the opportunity that had been afforded me to study in England, travel all over England and go to Paris, France. A friend of mine had also invited me to attend a convention in Spain. I have to keep reminding myself that none of this would have been possible if I was still using. Also, when I had returned from France I had received a letter from Kean stating that I had been inducted into the Epsilon Epsilon Omega Honor Society. I met a lady from South Africa and we became friends. She was telling me about what it was like to live in South Africa and about their customs and traditions.

Our class went on an excursion to the Royal Observatory in Greenwich. Then while there many of the students went to the line where if you put one foot on one side and another foot on the other side of the line you would be standing on different parts of the earth at the same time. This line separates the Western Hemisphere from the Eastern Hemisphere and the only place in the world that happens is at Greenwich. From the observatory you can see the Queen's house, the Naval College and the Maritime Museum. Also around this time I was granted an opportunity to attend the South African Freedom Day March and meet Nelson Mandela. At the march there were all kinds of bands and music and food from South Africa. Many of the people were dressed up in the kind of clothes they wear in South Africa. They also had people doing the various dances from South Africa. At the march I met two women from Johannesburg, South Africa and struck up an interesting conversation with them. I found out from them that the image we receive from the press of Winnie Mandela is quite different than how the people of Africa feel about her.

It is about time now to get ready to take my final exams and return to the United States. I am really feeling sad and depressed about having to leave England and the many friends I have made over here. The finals here are completely different than the finals in the states. Back home most of my exams are multiply choice, but in England the finals consist of ten questions and you have to answer two of them in essay form. Then I had to go to my twelve step meetings and say goodbye to all my new friends that

I had made over here. Many of them gave me their e-mail address and I have kept in contact with them when I came back to the states, until I had the fire and my address book with all my phone numbers, addressees, and e-mail addressees was destroyed. One of the members of the meetings I went to at night volunteered to give me a ride to the airport the day I was to leave. I remember before I left walking around town getting my last look of the town and getting down to the park where I had went many times to watch soccer games. I had no way to transport my television back home because when you fly from one country to another you are only allowed to carry a certain amount of weight. Therefore, I gave the television to my landlord. I remember feeling real sorry that I had to leave and even times now wishing I were in England. Now after going through all these feelings and emotions I came back to reality and realized that it was time to come back to the United States.

HANDLING THE HIGHS AND THE LOWS

I returned from England during the summer of 2002. I took the summer off to get ready for the fall semester going to Kean University as a graduate student. I went to the university to collect my various awards and plaques I had been awarded during the spring semester. Since I was not present during the presentation of these awards they were just collected and put in a box waiting for my return to the states. Even though I was returning from an experience of a lifetime I still had feelings of depression and low self worth. Part of the joy of receiving these awards was being presented them in the presence of your peers. I missed out in marching across the stage and receiving my degree in front of my family and friends and I still continued to attend my twelve step meetings once I returned home. I contacted the advisor of the New Jersey Student College Coalition and informed him that I was home and if there was anything I could do to be of service to the group just let me know.

The whole time I was in England I had paid my rent for my apartment in advance so I would have somewhere to live once I returned home. I had my cousin store my jeep in her garage during my absence. I began going back to church and becoming involved with the Sunday School program there.

There is another issue I need to discuss now. Part of the growing process for me, which I did extremely poor in was and still is dealing with my nieces. I have one that lives in New Jersey and the other one lives in North Carolina. When my brother was on his deathbed he asked me to look after his daughters and I agreed to. One of my biggest problems is my greed and not wanting to share things that were left to me. I would always say that I do not want to get to know them. The reason I use to say that was that they were not interested in knowing me except for what I was able to do for them. The truth is that both of them resemble my brother too much and looking at them was like looking at him. I decided why should I put myself through that. I know my cousin and aunt were disappointed in me because they would always ask me when was the last time I heard from my niece. I remember when my niece from North Carolina was graduating from college and getting married she had asked me to come down and see her. I really did not want to go but the only reason I went was that I didn't want to continually hear about it from my cousin and aunt. Then once my niece from North Carolina got married I figured I really didn't have to hear from her since she was married and it was her husband's responsibility to look after her. I recall on numerous times saying to her that I was not her father, and she remarked saying that she knew that. Even today I have a hard time when people say they love me, when they do not even know me. They only know what I have allowed them to see of myself. Even today as I am writing this account of my life it has been years since I have heard from them. Even though I think about them all the time my perception of myself and how I want people to perceive me has prevented me from trying to contact them and have a relationship with them. My cousin is always telling me that since I am single, with no children of my own and in very bad health that I should try and establish some sort of relationship with them, because you will never know when you will need somebody. My response has always been that since I am a veteran I can always go into a veteran's nursing home. I use that as an excuse to prevent myself from having to admit that just maybe I have been wrong about the way I have been treating people and have to apologize. It was also during this time that I had turned 50 years old and my church had given me a 50 year party in the church parking lot one Sunday after service. It really touched my heart. All the people there and the food and all the trouble that people had went out of their way to help me celebrate. People that I believed did not even like or speak to me was there wishing the best for me. It also helped me to understand that the way I perceive things is not necessarily the way things really are.

  The fall semester started and I got off to a good start. For the first time in a long time I was really starting to enjoy my life and the benefits that school had brought me. During this period of time I had received two of the highest medals that the state of New Jersey offers for my participation in the Viet Nam Conflict. Because I was the last remaining survivor I was presented a medal in behalf of my father for his participation in the landing in Normandy, France which brought a conclusion to World War II. Also, during this semester the local school newspaper had heard about me and did an interview with me entitled, "Gilchrist goes from most wanted to most respected". Another local newspaper did an article on me entitled "Somerville man becomes advocate for students in need". Earlier it had been suggested to me to start a scrapbook on myself with my various achievements and articles written about me and about this time I had accumulated about three scrapbooks. Many days when I find myself feeling sad and not good about myself I would look through my scrapbooks and some way they would miraculously lift up my spirits. I was still being involved with the Board of Directors I sat on for a local treatment center. During this time period I had applied for the Alumni Graduate Scholarship and was awarded the scholarship.

For one of my courses I had to do a project dealing with public administration and have an interview with a public official as part of that project. The project I chose was how the New Jersey Budget is put together. Once again everyone, including my professor, thought I was taking on more than I could handle. I already had some knowledge of how the budget worked due to my involvement in the past with the state legislature. I knew an Assemblyman who served on the Assembly Budget Committee and I contacted him and he said he would be more than willing to give me some time and help me with my project. It took about two separate interviews to get all the information I needed. I finished the paper and was given a very good grade plus some very good remarks concerning the information that I had researched. In November once again I went to the mayor's conference in Atlantic City. Every opportunity that was afforded me I would bring up the issue of Tuition Aid Grant for part time students. During this semester the New Jersey Student College Coalition had their annual conference and voted in a new administrative board. It was during this period of time that I decided it was time to let others run the group and just be there for moral support. I would go to the Commission of Higher Education meetings but would not speak. It was time to let others in executive positions step up. By taking this course of action I was able to put more attention into my schoolwork and maintain my honor roll status. It was during the winter recess that I took a trip for five days to Can Cun, Mexico. I really enjoyed myself being able to go on the beach in the morning in the peace and quiet and meditate. I came back and was ready to start the spring semester unknowing that my educational world was about to change.

I was just into the beginning of the spring semester when I had another seizure, which resulted in me contracting Bells Palsy. The Bells Palsy left the right side of my face paralyzed. I had to take physical therapy at the local veteran's hospital to regain normal use of my speech. I ended up missing the rest of that semester and was able to go back again in the fall. It was also at this time I was diagnosed with sleep apnea. I was constantly falling asleep in the daytime and went to the VA for treatment and they gave me a machine with a mask to use at nighttime. They informed me that at nighttime I have a tendency to stop breathing and this machine would help me. Also, I was given oxygen tanks to use to breath with at home because I was constantly out of breath and it was taking me forever to get from one point to another. So I usually had at least 13 tanks in my apartment. When in school I always had to take the elevators because I just couldn't handle walking the stairs. I was beginning to have problem with my two legs. For some reason they would swell up. Things had gotten so bad that when I went to Pathmark I had to use the cart to ride around in and get my groceries because I couldn't handle walking getting my groceries. While all this was going on I was still going to my twelve step meetings and staying clean. My weight had become so enlarged that I had a hard time in school finding a seat to sit in that was comfortable for the hours I would have to spend in that particular classroom. I was going to see a doctor for my health problems but things would continue to get progressively worse. I would find out that my diabetes was starting to have a negative effect on my kidneys.

 I stayed out of school for the rest of that spring semester and summer and prepared myself to start again in the fall. I had real high expectations for myself in the fall and the things I wanted to achieve academically. It seemed that things were going well for me that semester. I had my job as a graduate assistant at the university, my classes were going well and then **BAM** some people tried to kill me in November. I had signs on the front and back of my apartment stating that there was oxygen being used in the house and there was to be no trespassing and if I saw anyone on the property I would call the police. Because I use to sell drugs I knew what was going on. These young kids had the neighborhood seniors scared of them. They sold drugs and carried guns. I always remembered something I heard Dr. King say one time "***IF A MAN HASN'T FOUND SOMETHING WORTH DYING FOR THEN THAT MAN IS NOT FIT TO LIVE___***". I guess these kids thought I was joking, but they found out that I was deadly serious. So one night when I was sleeping I woke up to go to the bathroom and saw my kitchen and back porch in flames. First, I tried to get to the phone in the kitchen to call 911 but the intensity of the smoke was too strong. All I could think about was getting out of the house before the fire reached the oxygen tanks. There were some of my neighbors trying to put the fire out from the backyard. I had to yell at them to get away because if the fire reached the oxygen then that would be it. The police came and they questioned me. The police then took me to the hospital to have me checked out for smoke inhalation. Just to be sure they kept me over the night. When I was released in the morning I went back to see my apartment to sort things out and realized that it was a total loss. I talked to the fire marshall and he told me it was definitely arson. The fire marshall told me that the fire had been started on my back porch. One thing that really made me see just how valuable I treasured my life was in my apartment I have numerous awards, plaques, citations and medals that I had been awarded from various groups and organizations but when the fire broke out I did not think about any of them. All I thought about was getting myself out of there safely. It had taken me around nine years to accumulate everything I had in my apartment but I realized that all those things were just material possessions. I realized that as long as I had my life and health that I could regain those things if it was meant to be. As I looked around at the devastation and destruction that was facing me I also had to deal with the issue that there were people out there that were actually trying to kill me. I couldn't understand how my jeep was in front of the house and wasn't touched. For the first time in my life I was actually homeless. What was to happen to me next really brought home the understanding of what unconditional love was all about and that when you are trying to live a righteous life help comes from all unknown sources.

The things that I had been doing for people was not because I was looking for something in return, but because it was just the right thing to do. My aunt had told me to come and stay with her until I figured out what I was going to do. My landlord contacted me and told me that he realized that the fire was not my fault. My landlord told me that he had another apartment in another part of town that he had promised to someone else but if I wanted it I could have it. In the meetings that I go to at night one of their suggestions is that you avoid people, places and things that you were associated with during your using days. In the most part I took their suggestion to heart and practiced them, but there was this one individual that I remained friends with even though his lifestyle might not have been compatible to mine. We had always been there for one another. When he was in the hospital in New York I would drive out there every day to see him. When I had gotten stabbed and came home he would stop by my house everyday to see if there was anything that I needed. Well, when it came time to move into my new apartment him and his brother went over to the old apartment and whatever wasn't completely destroyed by the fire they moved for me. I need to say that also at this time I was in and out of hospitals a lot and the new apartment that I had was on the third floor. They moved the stuff up there for me and told me I need to rest and take it easy. The stuff that they moved was not just light stuff. They moved a brand new brass bed that I had just recently purchased, my exercise bike and treadmill and charged me basically nothing for doing it.

The local paper in town had written an article about the fire and had referred to me as an "activist". I had never thought of myself in those terms. I had went to the local Red Cross for some aid and was told to remain there because this lady that I knew that works for the county wanted to see me. When she saw me she started hugging me and crying and I told her I was all right. I remember when she told me how she had told her husband about it and that I was all right and that she was the one that was all messed up. Then she took me out clothes shopping because the only clothes I had were the ones that were on my back. I was really touched about how people were really reaching out to aid me in my time of direst. The main thing that kept going through my mind was the fact that at my twelve step meetings I go to they always focus on the fact that I shouldn't use no matter what. Now was the time for me to apply that concept.

One of the local politicians in the community that I had become friends with when he read about the fire had left messages around town that he wanted to see me. When I contacted him he told me he had a dinette set with chairs that I could have. If you were to see it you could tell that it was a very expensive piece of furniture. What really surprised me was people have this illusionary belief that politicians really do not do hard physical work. That belief was destroyed when I saw this politician along with a friend of mine, carrying this table to my third floor apartment. Next I had a message from my local assemblyman and when I went to see him he presented me a check to help me rebuild. I had been involved with this program which took a year to complete in the past. That program was designed to help teach certain individuals about the county we lived in and the various services available to them. In that program I had met various individuals from various segments and levels of the county. When they heard about the fire they were contacting me and asking what was it that they could do to help me out.

The spring semester was just starting and things seemed to get better after everything that I had been going through. Also, about this time the monthly income that I had been receiving since my mother passed was about to end. Now I found myself in another dilemma. I had to find another source of income. I have to thank my good friend who moved to

Las Vegas for the solution to this dilemma. For years she had been telling me that I should go and file for social security. So right before the fire I had went to the social security office and applied for SSI. Also I applied for non-service connected disability insurance with the government. It would take me about a year before I would start collecting the disability insurance, but luckily I would receive the SSI just when my other source of income was to end. So things were starting to look up for me and I was working real hard at maintaining a positive state of mind. I was looking forward to going to my classes and I still had my job on campus as a graduate assistant.

One morning I woke up and was taking a shower and was continually falling down. I was having a seizure. I was able to call 911 and wait for the ambulance to come and take me to the hospital. On one of the falls I had injured my left leg and forearm. I remember calling my cousin and her telling me to just stay on the floor until the ambulance arrived. I was taken to the local hospital and after being there for a few weeks they told me that they wanted to transfer me to a rehabilitation center for more intense therapy. I agreed to go. Once I arrived at the rehabilitation center for the first couple of weeks I wasn't able to start right away because they were having a hard time regulating my blood pressure. They would not allow me to participate in the therapy sessions until they were able to control my blood pressure. Also, while there they changed a lot of my medicine including my seizure medication (which I would find out later would have disastrous effects on me). Once my therapist had did everything they could for me it was time to release me. One of the things they told me was that I need to look for an apartment on a lower level and that I really shouldn't be living alone. As far as the living alone was concerned I had no choice because I couldn't afford to live anyplace else. My social worker there arranged for me to have a visiting nurse and physical therapist come by three times a week to work with me.

I was released and went home. I was really missing not being able to go to school but also realized that I needed to get my health in order. Also, at this time because of my health issues I was unable to go to my meetings as regularly as I would have like to. Things were progressing for the better for me. I was having my regular visits by the visiting nurse and physical therapist and making my appointments at the local VA hospital.

A few weeks after I had returned home I had went to Sunday school and Church and wasn't really feeling too well. I left church early to stop by Pathmark to get something to eat before I went home. At this time when I went to Pathmark I was still using the rider they provide for people who have a hard time walking. I was still using the oxygen tanks to breathe off and on. While in Pathmark I started having chest pains and they called the ambulance and once again I was headed back to the hospital. I was still using the same medication that the people at the rehabilitation facility had prescribed for me to take. A lot of the previous medication that I had been taking they had stopped. While I was in the hospital this time it was revealed to me that I suffer from congestial heart failure. Now I had that to add on to all the other things I had going wrong with me health wise, but I also realized that what I was going through was due to my own fault. I had to remember that when I was using it I who made the decision to stop taking insulin for my diabetes for two years. It was I who was eating out of garbage cans and who knows what diseases and germs I was willingly putting inside of my body. I understood that using would not solve the problem but only add on to it. So I decided to focus my attention on what I needed to do to get better. For the first time in a long time I was willing to listen to what my doctors had to say and take it to heart. For the first time I really made a decision to stick to the diet they had me on. For the first time I was taking my medicine when it was suppose to be taken and not when I felt like taking it. For the first time I really decided to exercise on a regular basis and try and lose weight.

When I came home from the hospital I was still having problems with the swelling of my legs. I would go to the hospital every three or four weeks and stay in there for a few days so they could drain excess fluid from my legs. The last time I was in the hospital having fluid drained from my legs I went through an experience like I had never had before. I do not recall exactly what happened and all the information I have concerning it is what my doctor's and nurses have revealed to me. I was in a room with this other patient and when I woke up I was in a room by myself. My arms and legs were shackled to the bed. Later on I was told that I had a Grand Mall Seizure. A Grand Mall Seizure is the worse kind of seizure you can or want to have. You are totally unconscious and have no knowledge of what is going on around you or what you are doing. I was told they had four security guards in there trying to hold me down and that wasn't working. Due to the fact that I had become so violent they had to paralyze me. Once I was paralyzed they had a tube inserted in my mouth so I wouldn't choke on my tongue and they connected this bag in me for when I had to go to the bathroom. I do not recall any of these things being done to me.

I guess I was in a state of unconsciousness for a few days and when I finally came out of it I was still paralyzed and my arms and legs were still shackled to the bed. It was the worse feelings in the world. I was paralyzed from the neck on down. Eventually, I would be able to wiggle my feet, then my fingers but in the meantime I was chained down and unable to move or communicate. I couldn't communicate to them that I was hungry or thirsty, I just had to lay there in the same position unable to move or anything. I remember praying to God to either let me come out of this or to let me die. I didn't want to live the rest of my life in that kind of state. I believe God heard my prayers because eventually he had me come out of it. It wasn't funny then but now when I think about it I see it as amusing.

    A nurse had come in to take my blood pressure and had asked the other nurses to come into the room with her. I guess she had heard about how violent I was before. My doctors came in and said it was all right to remove the restraints, and the nurses argued strongly against it. They told my doctors that they were not here the night before when they had to go through all that hell trying to control me and calm me down. You could look in their eyes and see real fear or serious hesitation. Evidentially, though they were able to remove things from my body and their courage became stronger and they were willing to come in and do what they needed to do. When they would come in to take my blood pressure and my arms would jerk you could see that they were ready to fly out of the room. With one eye they would be looking at my arm and the blood pressure equipment and the other eye they had it attached to my eyes to make sure there wasn't any sudden change.

    As I started to get better and was able to speak more and more my doctors told me they believed the reason I had this Grand Mall Seizure was because of the change of seizure medication that I had been put on when I was in the rehabilitation center. They told me they were putting me back on my old seizure medication and that I should stay on it. They also emphasized the importance of my not living alone and finding myself an apartment on the first level that was without steps. They were saying I was lucky this time because I was in the hospital when I had my Grand Mall Seizure, but what would happen to me if I had been home alone and had one.

    I need to say that at this time the only people that I let know I was in the hospital was my aunt and cousins. I think it goes back to when I was a small boy and my father had told me if you want to cry I'll give you something to cry about. Then I promised myself I would never let anyone see me cry or see me in a vulnerable state and I think that is part of the reason why I will not let people know when I am in the hospital. I would inform them once I got home. When I came home my doctors told me they didn't want me to drive for six months until I had six months free from seizure activity. I think I have amazed people that I can have my jeep right there in the parking lot with the keys to it and not touch it.

I realized though it is not just my life that is at jeopardy, it is the lives of other innocent people on the roads. When I had to have my jeep have some brake work done I paid to have it towed to the shop, caught a taxi to take me to the shop and pay the bill and then had to pay it towed backed home. In my meetings they emphasized how important it is not to partake in that negative behavior no matter what. Therefore, I told myself that I was not going to drive for six months no matter what. So everywhere I went I was catching trains, buses or taxies.

A few months later I had received word from the veteran's administration that they had made a decision on my application for disability benefits and had ruled in my favor. Now that this was one less thing I had to worry about I found myself in a position where I could work on my future and how I could better serve myself and mankind. I found myself with a lot of time on my hands and was seriously able to think about the fire and how I had arrived at that state in life where people would want to kill me. I was able to think about if I had the chance to do it all over again would I do it the same way or do things differently. I believe that things happen to us for a specific reason. I also believe there is a reason why some people are left out in the streets in their addiction to go through the abuse and degradation that goes with that lifestyle. I also believe there is a reason why some of us are saved from having to continually live in that lifestyle. I truly believe that the change that happened in my life was only through the grace and intervention of someone who had no other reason to do it but that they loved me. If I had the chance to relive the series of events that led up to the fire would I still call the police. Yes, I would. Like I quoted earlier from Dr. King, ***"ANY MAN WHO HASN'T FOUND SOMETHING WORTH DYING FOR THAT MAN ISN'T FIT TO LIVE".*** I truly believe how could I really appreciate a good car if I had never had a lemon before. How could I really appreciate a fine steak dinner if I had never eaten out of garbage cans before? How could I enjoy the beauty in life today if I have never experienced the ugliness that life could bring to me? How could I appreciate a good relationship if I have never been in bad relationships before, and how could I appreciate the good times if I had never went through times of utter desperation and degradation? Finally, how could I appreciate the person I am today if I never gave myself the chance and opportunity to get to know who I am? Yes, I understand how these things evolved into this act of violence against me, but if they hadn't happen how could I enjoy my life today.

AND YOU THOUGHT YOU COULDN'T CHANGE

I remember believing all my life that people were pre destined to do and become what they were destined to become and that there was no way to change or break the mode. I no longer believe in that concept. I believe in that old saying *"that whatever the mind conceive it can achieve."*

Yes, if I can change anyone can change. I also learned at the same time that no one can do or live in this life all by his or her self. The most important thing is to believe in one's self. Regardless of how much others say we are worthless, we will never become anything worthwhile, but a complete waste of human life until we believe that we can do and become anything we want to. I have learned in this life to never let anyone talk me out of my dreams, ambitions or willingness to grow. In the end what really matters is being able to go to bed at night and look myself in the mirror and feel good about the person I am and the things I have done. Realizing that doing a good thing is not necessarily the right thing to do, but the right thing to do is do the things for my fellow man that I would want my fellow man to do for me.

As I have mentioned numerous times in this manuscript I am an avid believer in the philosophies and concept of the late Rev. Dr. Martin Luther King, Jr. and as I close I would like to quote something that I feel sums up what I hope my life has been a representation of. That statement is *"If you want to be important—wonderful. If you want to be great— wonderful. But recognize that he who is greatest among you shall be your servant. The thing I like about this definition of greatness is it means that everybody can be great because everybody can serve. You don't have to have a college degree to serve. You don't have to be able to make your subject or verb agree to serve. You don't have to know about Plato and Aristotle to serve. You don't have to know Einstein's theory of relativity to serve. You don't have to know about the second theory of thermodynamics to serve. All you need is a heart full of grace (grace is defined as something given to someone who needs not to), a soul generated by love, and you can be that servant."*

Then he goes on to talk about his death and his funeral and says; *"Every now and then I guess we all think realistically about that day when we will all be victimized with what is life's final common denominator—that something we call death. We all think about it. And every now and then I think about my own death and I think about my own funeral. And I don't think about it in a morbid sense. And every now and then I ask myself, "What is it that I would want said?"* His response to that question is *" If any of you are around when I have to meet my day, I don't want a long funeral. And if you get somebody to deliver the eulogy, tell them not to talk to long. And every now and then I wonder what I want them to say. Tell them not to mention that I have a Nobel Peace Prize—that isn't important. Tell them not to mention that I have three or four hundred other awards—that's not important. Tell them not to mention where I went to school."* For me this is the most important part of his speech and how I would want people to remember me. Not the person I use to be or the things I use to do but the person I was at the time of my death. *"I'd like somebody to mention that Martin Luther King, Jr. tried to give his life serving others. I'd like for somebody to say that day that Martin Luther King., tried to love somebody. I want you to say that I tried to right on the war question. I want you to be able to say that day that I did try and feed the hungry. I want you to be able to say that day I did try in my life to clothe those that were naked. I want you to say that I tried to love and serve humanity.*

These thoughts were running through my mind that night my apartment was on fire and I was running out of there trying to save my life. All the various awards and college degrees and articles written about me that were framed and placed all over my apartment just didn't seem that important. Even when I came home from the hospital the next day my mind was not on retribution or revenge but on how I could continue to serve mankind with whatever time I had remaining on earth.

I have heard it said many times before if all the suffering one person goes through just helps one person from having to go through all the degradation and dereliction an individual goes through in addiction then all the suffering is worth it. It took a long time to evolve into believing in a concept like that. But I truly hope and believe if this book helps just one person from going through what I went through then the pain was all worth it. The final thought I want to leave you with is if this individual can go from being a high school dropout to studying at one of the finest universities in the world, if he can go from being dispised by everyone to being respected by everyone, if he can go from hating himself to loving himself then ***"YOU CAN TOO"***

FEAR OF INTIMACY

Sitting here all alone thinking of my past and present life I am pondering the reason behind why do I always find myself by myself. At times I have believed it was hereditary. I remember after my father had died it was just my mother and myself. I remember during this time period my mother had basically isolated herself from the rest of the world. She only left the house when she had to go shopping or go to the bank or work in her garden. Other than that she stayed in the house. What is it about intimacy that scares people so much? Merriam-Webster's Collegiate Dictionary describes intimacy as **" belonging to or characterized one's deepest nature, marked by very close association, contact, or familiarity. Marked by a warm friendship developed through long association."** I remember one time hearing someone describe intimacy as **"In to me I see."**

As I think about intimacy I keep coming up with the question **"Why am I so afraid of letting people get to know me or more important why am I so afraid of letting Andre know Andre."** The answer has to lie within my own self. I remember hearing once that if you have no acceptance of yourself then any acceptance will do. I remember the other day I was talking to a friend of mine on the phone and she had asked me about explaining some information for her and wanted to come over to my apartment As much as I loved the idea of having a female alone in my apartment there was also a great amount of fear involved with having someone alone in my apartment Where did this fear come from? How did this fear manifest itself into a lifestyle that would eventually have a controlling role on how I would live my life today? As in the Part One "You Thought You Couldn't Change Either" the answer to these questions must lie within my life's story.

HOW IT ALL STARTED

    I remember growing up and noticing that even though my parents loved one another there was not a great deal of intimacy involved. Even though they discussed everything that was to affect my brother and myself there was no intimacy involved as a family unit. There was no holding of hands or verbal expressions of love within the family unit. My father came from a school of thought that believed actions spoke louder than words. Rather than say I love you I will show you be making sure you always have a roof over your head, that there was always food in the house for you to eat and providing all the other necessary elements that make life worth living. I think that part of the problem was that my father came from a school of thought that believed that showing emotions was a weakness. Especially at this time in American history Afro American men had to portray this image of undue strength and no vulnerability because if you showed any signs of weakness people would take advantage of you. I think this is why at this time when my father went to discipline me and I started crying he would remark that he was going to give me something to cry about. This is why at this time I made a promise to myself that no one would ever see me cry again, regardless of how much pain I was going through inside.

    Growing up as a young teen-ager one of the biggest drives in my life was that of self-acceptance. Because I felt that people could and would not accept me as I was was due in part to the fact that I had no acceptance of myself. I think that the major reason for that was that I had no faith or belief in myself. Part of that reasoning was in response to my physical characteristics. Being Afro-American I already believed I was starting off behind everyone else. Then taking a look at the fact that I have always been overweight, not particular nice looking you develop a case of low self esteem and find yourself willing to do anything to be accepted by your peers. I remember a particular event that happened to me when I was extremely young. I believe I was around 8 to 10 years old and one of my favorite things to watch on television was the original Superman series. I have heard this said many times and I really identify with it how fantasy was a lot of peoples first drug of choice. I really identify with that because I never felt satisfied within my own body. I always felt if I could just be someone else I would have a much easier time in succeeding in this life. So I remember this one-day I had tied my bathrobe around my neck and went to the end of my bed and jumped off pretending I could fly like Superman. I ended up hitting the other end of the bed and breaking my nose. There was a lesson to be learned here but I did not learn it until much later on in life. That lesson is when you try to be anything or anyone other than who you are or whom God made you to be disastrous things will happen to you.

As I continued to age I was becoming more involved in my environment. I found out the further I moved away from the person I was born to be the more I was becoming the person people expected me to become. It is apparent to me today how I allowed so many golden opportunities I had to know myself slip away. I was becoming the person that is so often referred to as Dr. Jeckyl and Mr. Hyde. For those of you who are not familiar with the story of Dr. Jeckyl and Mr. Hyde let me sum it up for you very quickly. It supposedly took place in London, England and was about a doctor who was trying to find a cure for why people behave the way they do and came up with this formula in the form of a drink. He needed someone to drink it and test it so he tested it on himself. Once the liquid was inside of him he would turn into someone completely different than the doctor who was trying to find a remedy for mental illness. The funny thing about me was that at an early age I didn't need any substance or liquid for this transformation to take place. As I continually aged I found myself needing to put some sort of substance in my body to cause this transformation. As time went on I found myself needing to take more and more, not necessarily for the transformation but to just to be able to function. I finally arrived at the stage where Mr. Hyde was seldom around and Dr. Jeckyl was living with me 24 hours a day and my only concern was to do whatever was necessary to continually make Dr. Jeckyl feel good.

I recall that around this time I was very active in my local church. I was going to Sunday School and Church services each Sunday with my brother and father. It was being instilled inside of us certain spiritual values and morals that would make life so much easier to live by. But that would not be the case. My adventure into the life of fantasy would continue to increase and increase. Eventually, I reached the point where Andre no longer ceased to exist and I had no idea who the person in this body was.

A LIFE OF FANTASY

Webster's defines fantasy as **"the power or process of creating unrealistic or improbable mental images in response to psychological needs."** In lay man terms it is the process which allows an individual to survive in his present environment by allowing that individual to become someone entirely different from who he actually is. I had reached a point in my young life where I was so desperate for acceptance that I was willing to forsake all values and morals I had been taught. I had reached a stage in my life where the only time I felt good about myself was when I was being completely different than the person I was raised to be. As I would continue to age, unknowing to myself, this new version of Andre would take over complete control of my life. It wouldn't be until years, many years later that the real Andre would begin to emerge. As I look back the first stage in this redevelopment was the creation of someone identical to my brother. I would buy the same type of clothes he would wear; I would get the same type of haircuts he would get. I would listen to him talk to women on the phone and then call someone up and try to impersonate and emulate him on the phone with them. I never understood the concept that by being myself people would accept me for who I was and not the person they perceived I was or the person I was trying to become. I never understood the true meaning of humility being that people would accept me for the person I was and not inspite of the person I wasn't. I reached a point in my life when I would see a female and the only reason I would show any interest in her had to be because she was the type of woman my brother would go out with. I recalled during this period if I saw someone I was interested in first I had to get the approval of my brother, and if I ceased to get his approval I would not bother with that female. Around this time the big thing was to go out with Caucasian women, and I really did not actively take part in that behavior until I saw my brother involved in it. As we talk about "intimacy or in to me I see" I remember I was not that much interested in the mixing of the races but if it was all right with my brother then it couldn't be all that bad.

I recall as I was growing up I would engage in certain behaviors due to the self imposed pressure I put on myself to be accepted by those around me regardless of how I felt about myself. Because I never felt good about the person I was inside I was willing to adapt other people's values and morals and then wonder why I never felt fulfilled when I was alone by myself. Earlier we talked about Dr. Jeckle and Mr. Hyde and how they manifested into the type of person I had to live with for quite a while. Let me give you three prime examples of what I am talking about. First, the guys that I ran around with had this game to test one's courage and strength. Two men would put one of their feet alongside of the other person's foot and then they would take turns exchanging punches into each other's chest. The first person to move their foot or body back was considered the loser and having no strength or courage to endure this. Now because I wanted to be accepted so badly by this group of people many days I went home with extremely sore chest. My wanting to be accepted as someone I wasn't was so deep I remember many days I would ask my brother at home to practice punching me in the chest just so I would be ready when we ran into our peer group. Another test we had was something we called knuckles. It was a card game and the end result was the number of cards you lost by was the number of times you had to have your knuckles hit by each member who was playing the game. Now each person would take and hold all 52 cards in their hand and take turns hitting the person who lost the number of times they lost by. Many days I remember going home with my knuckles all bloody and sore, but the satisfaction I believed I had was as least they knew I could take it.

Other experiences that I experienced reminds me how this principle of intimacy has never been a real important aspect of my life. Part of the necessary details of the principle of intimacy is being able to look inside myself and deciding on the type of person I want to be. Once that decision is made I need to be vigilant in all aspects of that decision. I remember growing up at a time when there were a lot of conflicts between the races. I remember finding myself caught up in this internal dilemma. My father was a Christian and religious and made my brother and me attend Sunday School and Church. My father believed in the doctrines of the Rev. Dr.

Martin Luther King, Jr. that was of non-violence. I remember listening and believing in those doctrines and then going out in the streets and at that same time believing in the doctrines of Malcolm X, the Muslims, The Black Panthers, Huey Newton, Eldridge Cleaver, Angela Davis and so on. So you could see this internal battle going on inside of me of who I really wanted to be. I had lost myself so long ago that I needed validation from anyone to make me feel good about myself. I remember my father had taken me to Washington, DC to see the March on Washington. Now there was someone else for me to emulate rather than working on the concept of "In To Me I See." I remember my father would have a lot of records around the house of Dr. King and I would memorize them and run around the house preaching out sermons like I was Dr. King. I remember especially the day he was killed. I remember talking to some friends on the phone and they told me the next day when they went to school anyone white they were going to punch. I remember participating in that behavior because rather than having the moral fortitude to stand on my own convictions I needed to do what ever was necessary to be considered a part of. Regardless of what the consequences might be. I remember going to school that next day and hitting anyone white regardless of whether they were male, female, or teacher. I rationalize to myself so I could live with that behavior that anyone who was white and had any bit of sense wouldn't come to school today after what happened yesterday. Even today as I am starting to get to know and like who I am I have guilt and remorse feelings about those actions and behaviors I participated in. All because I refused to allow me to get to know myself. Even today I have not been able to watch the movie Roots because I am not sure on my feelings and reactions to watching some of the things that I know actually went on.

FANATSY TURNS INTO A WAY OF LIVING

As I continued to age I found myself moving further away from reality and going deeper into this fanatical vision of self. In an attempt not to know self or get to know self I found myself putting other people on these unrealistic pedalstools and transfer what I perceived to be my worthless life into their life of adventure and excitement. What I didn't realize then was that I was sentencing myself to a self made prison and that it would take years of degradation and dereliction and untold pain and misery before I would have the willingness and strength to look for the answers to my life from God and inside myself.

My inability to take advantage of many of the opportunities that this life had afforded me is a direct result of living my life to impress others. I remember my father affording me this golden opportunity to attend this private school in South Carolina. Instead of taking advantage of this opportunity all I could think about was transferring my brother from up in New Jersey down to South Carolina in the shape of my body. When I first arrived there I was real fearful and afraid because I didn't know anyone and there was no one there to tell me what to do so I wouldn't have to take responsibility for my own actions. Upon arriving there I found out that the students there had this perception of what people were the North were like and because of the things they had read about people from New Jersey, New York and Pennsylvania a great majority of them were leery of me. Once again I had a golden opportunity to get outside of myself and pretend to be someone I really wasn't. I even took this role to a point where I basically threatened the school's president. I had reached a point where I was just being disruptive, non-responsive to the schools rules and guidelines. I remember finally getting to the point where the school president had called me into his office and informed me that he had just got off the phone with my father and had received permission to discipline me. You need to understand that at this time in our nation teachers were allowed to physically discipline their students. Upon hearing this news I immediately let the president know that he needs to remember where I am from. I also informed him that if he thinks I am just going to stand here and let him discipline me and do nothing he was crazy. After much more thought he thought he would be to everyone's benefit for me to return home to New Jersey. The result was that was what I wanted. I was so excited about going home and being with my brother it didn't matter to me what my father would do to me for being expelled. Today I am able to look back with regret and see this golden opportunity I had thrown away but because of my unwillingness and inability to look inside myself and realize that I was no better or worse than anyone else regardless of my physical attributes and how I believed that people perceived me.

The rest of my adolescence childhood was riveted with more experiences like the above mentioned one. My father believed that education was the best way to gain economic freedom. That didn't concern me. The only thing that was of extreme importance to me was being around the one person I wanted to be like. If I saw a female that I was interested being involved with I first needed to gain my brother's approval. If he didn't give his approval that was good enough for me not to have anything to do with the female. This unwillingness to get to know myself and to pursue things that would be in the best interest of myself led me into a way of life that I was not raised or taught to endeavor in.

Another incidence that shows the consequences when one fails to know one self and allows other to be the driving force in their lives happened during the times in our countries history when there was a lot of racial unrest throughout the nation. During this time following the death of Dr. King's assassination many of the other black organizations beliefs were opposite that of Dr. King's. They really used this opportunity to explain how non-violence doesn't work and how a man whose whole life was based on non-violence died a violent death. These groups such as the Black Muslims, the Black Panthers; people such as Malcolm X, Huey Newton, Bobby Seals, Eldridge Cleaver, Angela Davis etc. were taking this opportunity to get many of the minority citizens in the country to take to heart the belief that the only way they would get what was rightfully due them was by taking it by any means necessary. As I had stated earlier when you have no acceptance then any acceptance will do and you will do whatever you think will have other people accept you. Even though I had been raised and brought up listening to the concepts and beliefs of Dr. King and his non violent approach to life I started to accept this new concept of life even though I did not believe in it at all. So during this time of civil unrest around the country blacks were raising up and rioting all over the country. There were riots in the South, Watts in California, Detroit, Washington, DC, Philadelphia, Harlem in New York, and finally here at home in New Jersey. At the same time that they had a riot in Newark and Plainfield, New Jersey a riot broke out here in my hometown of Somerville, New Jersey. I explicitly remember going to a town meeting held at a local fire station to discus some of the local problems we were having in our community as far as funds being used to uplift the Caucasian community and nothing going to build up the minority population. I remember someone yelling out if you are not willing to use the funds to help build up all aspects of the community then you can use the money to rebuild the community. As I reflect on this I think of the part I would ultimately play in it. Due to my lack of knowing of one's self, the inability to live my life with some sort of integrity (constant application of spiritual principles regardless of the circumstance), the inability to live my life by my own sense of morals and values and goals I ended up participating in actions that even today I do not approve of. I think of the fact that if I did not engage in this behavior that my fear of intimacy would have allowed myself to get to know exactly what it was I wanted out of life and that it would have given me the strength to stand on my own two feet regardless of what people around me were doing. I think back to when people would eventually leave that firehouse and headed straight for the business district of the town. Upon reaching the town people would commence to breaking windows and looting and stealing and the physical infliction that was put on people just because of the color of their skin was different than ours. Yes, I took part in this activity even though it really wasn't the person I was inside or the person I was raised to be but the fear deep inside was so strong of what would my peers say if they did not see me participating in this outrageous behavior.

TRANSITION INTO DR. JECKLE AND MR. HYDE

As I look back into the various experiences and events that occurred in my childhood I notice a transformation that was taking place without my consent. Because of my unwillingness to look inside myself and discover who exactly I was and what were the pieces of the puzzle that put me together which made me the unique person I was I found myself going through this transformation and exhibiting characteristics flaws that I saw so demeaning in other people. I was constantly drinking the drink of acceptance by any means necessary, the drink of giving in to peer pressure, the drink of transforming oneself from that of low self-esteem, low self-worth to that of what I perceived I needed to be to be accepted by those I looked up to.

Even at an early age I found myself needing to be someone else in situations when it came to dealing with the other sex. I felt so uncomfortable with myself due to my physical characteristics and my speech impediment I needed to reach outside of myself just to engage in conversations with them. I recall feeling so inhibited by my own inadequacies that I would spend hours at home in the bathroom just practicing what I would say if I just happen to run into someone the next day. I remember listening to records by the top recording artist of the time and then using some of their lines when I would write letters to women. I remember doing things to degrade women and feeling ashamed and guilty about it but my feelings of being accepted were more important than how I felt about myself after I did some of these things. Eventually as I was doing these things more and more I was finding it a lot easier to live with myself and ignore the feelings of guilt and shame. This transformation would follow me right into the service and stay with me right through my active addiction. It wouldn't be until I started going to these meetings at night and did some introspective work on myself that Dr. Jeckle would disappear and Andre would once again appear.

To get a real good look and understanding of how this fear of intimacy really affected me in the areas of relationships it is necessary to take a deep down look at these relationships and see what they were really made of. I remember hearing at my first rehab how can you have respect and dignity for someone else when you have none for yourself. I think of the definition of the word integrity, which I have heard defined as the constant application of spiritual principles regardless of the circumstances. I see today that in my developing years in my childhood I had no respect, dignity or integrity for myself. My spiritual principles were composed of what the people in my peer group were. The thing that what bothers me the most today is that there was no excuse for my behavior of women. I had a perfect example at home. I saw how my father treated my mother with the utmost respect and dignity. How her opinion was just as important as his own and maybe just maybe at times he would be wrong and she was right. Then having the ability to admit when he was wrong and ask to be forgiven. I remember even today something my cousin told me in my active addiction that she has always loved me but there was a period of time she did not like me. The way I treated women like a piece of meat and when I was done discarded them. I was not raised to treat women that way, but like I mentioned before when Dr. Jeckle took over the person I was inside I wasn't operating on my own will power. At the same time I can honestly say that there was still a measure of human decency and compassion in me. There were areas of my soul that Dr. Jeckle hadn't reached yet. There was one instance when I went to the hospital with my brother because his first daughter was being born. We were in the labor room where his girlfriend was in labor. Now anyone who has been blessed to witness the beauty of childbirth can attest to the pain and suffering that some women go through. My brother found this amusing. I remember him laughing and saying she doesn't look all that tough now. I remember looking at her and seeing and hearing the pain she was going through. I couldn't stand it. I left the hospital. I remember when I say my brother later on he asked my why I left and I told him he might have found that amusing but I didn't and I wouldn't take part in his insensity towards another human being. Regardless though of what I thought about the way my brother treated women I wanted to be just like him. I just didn't have the internal makeup so I found myself at times forcing myself to do things that ultimately were far worse than any of the things I saw my brother do.

Another situation allowed me to see that there was still some measure of hope in me and that I wasn't totally devoid of any human empathy or kindness for people of the opposite sex. This happened at a time when I was selling drugs and before I actually began to use my own product. There was this girl that I had always liked from the time we were in school together but due to my lack of self worth and self-confidence I believed she would never want to have anything to do with me. Plus, my brother had also told me that she was out of my league. At this time she was heavy into using drugs and was at a point where her drug use was more than what she could afford. I use to love to find women in this situation because then I could always use my drugs for sex. So I went about my process of setting her up by giving her some free stuff and knowing her financial situation I let her know the rest of the stuff I had I had to sell. Immediately the proposal came about. For some reason, which I can not explain I couldn't go through with it. As much as I wanted to be with her I didn't want it to be about the drugs. I wanted it to be about the fact that she wanted to be with me because of who I was and not what I had to offer her. I gave her few extra bottles and left. There was another instance where there was another girl I had went to school with and she was pregnant and I knew she was due within the next few days. She came to me looking to buy some drugs. I told myself if she didn't buy the drugs from me she would just go to someone else so I might as well get the money. For years I use this to rationalize and make it possible for me to live with myself. I didn't want to look at the fact that I might be contributing to the destruction of another human life. One more case involved me using my drugs to have sex with women. There was this one girl who was the girlfriend of a friend of mine who I happened to know at that time had a drug habit. When I came into town and she saw me she invited me to come over to her apartment with the pretense that she wanted to buy some drugs from me. What it came right down to was that she didn't have any money and wanted to trade sex for drugs. Of course I went along with it. Today we label these women doing these kind of things with negative descriptions, but what about the men who also engage in these activities just for instant gratification. The fear of intimacy begins with the lack of respect and commitment to one self. It wasn't until I started to take a deep look at myself and admitted to myself that this is not the type of life I was raised to live or wanted to live. It wasn't until I was willing to admit to myself that these actions were based on the premises that due to the lack of self esteem I had that only women with major drug problems was the only way a women would want to engage in sexual activities with me. It wasn't until I took a deep look inside myself and admitted to myself that if I wanted to be in a wholesome relationship that I needed to work on the qualities within myself that would make me somebody that someone would want to be in a relationship with me. It wasn't until I internalized the belief that I deserved the best in life and not what I thought money could purchase. I had to realize that there were some people who were more impressed with the inside of someone than their outside. I had to stop questioning people's motives and take some people on face value. I needed to start incorporating values such as trust and faith into my life. I needed to stop saying I believe in God when my actions were of a completely different nature. My actions needed to show that if I wanted to be in a committed relationship with someone then I needed to work on the qualities within myself that would attract someone to want to be in a relationship with me. Until I was willing to incorporate all these concepts into my life then there would be no chance of intimacy. I've heard someone say something one time that has always stayed and made a lasting impression on me **"I want to stand you up before I lay you down."** Part of my fear of intimacy in relation to women was that if they really knew the person I really am they would either reject or use my vulnerability for their own personal benefit. I needed to understand that I needed to stop trying to live my life in a manner to protect myself from what I possibly conceived might cause me undue pain, misery and suffering. I needed to realize that what ever is going to happen is going to happen and that even with pain there is a lesson to be learned. I recall telling people how can they know if they are in a good relationship if they have never been in a bad relationship. How could they know if they have a good car if they have never experienced bad cars? How could they appreciate joy if they have never gone through sadness? Now I found myself needing to take these principles and apply them to my own life. It wouldn't be until I was willing to do these things that I had any chance of getting rid of Dr. Jeckle forever and take the time to get to know and appreciate Andre.

DEVELOPMENT OF INTIMACY

What must I do today to change my life around? What must I do today if I want people's perception of me to change? What must I do to achieve the benefits of intimacy or In To Me I See? In the development of intimacy one of the first criteria's' for that process to begin is self-honesty. Before I can be honest with anyone about whom I am with my various strengths and weaknesses I must be able to admit them to myself. As I have been writing this much thought has been going into my life and the way I have been perceived by others, especially family members, and what part I myself have played in developing and cultivating that perception. I was thinking about when some members of my family have died and I have not been contacted and informed about it. I remember shortly after my mother died that her younger sister passed away. It was about a year after the funeral that I had found out about my aunt's death. I was told that the reason I was not told was that they thought I didn't really care and wouldn't have come to the funeral. I informed them that whatever they thought about the reason why I do the things I do I would have went, if only for the fact that was my mother's sister. My aunt would come up and visit my mother and I looked forward to her trips up here. Recently, I had an aunt that had moved down South quite a few years ago and it was just recently that I had heard that she had been sick for a while. About a month ago she passed away and it was only a few days ago I heard about it. I would have gone to the funeral but people once again believed they knew how I would respond in certain situations. I remember when they were living up here and my father was still alive one of his traditions was on Christmas Day and New Years Day he would take my brother and myself around visiting our relatives. I use to look forward to doing that. I was a good friend with her children and many times I would go over to their house on my own because I enjoyed being around them. They had a family business that ran a service station and many days I would go to the shop just to hang out with them. Then recently, one of her sons who are currently living up here had remarried and became a deacon in his church. I didn't even know he was going to church. I always thought that we had remained close. Many times when I was in town I would stop by the shop to see how he is doing. It hurt me inside that all these things were going on and that I was not being a part of it just because people believed they knew what my reactions would be. Once again I had to think of the part I played in cultivating those beliefs. Then I remembered when my mother died people would come around the house to see me and I would look out the window and if they didn't have anything in their hands I would not let them in. So I had to ask myself if they were really the blame or do I need to look inside myself for the blame. In order to survive on the streets during my active addiction I needed to portray the role of an unfeeling, insensitive human being. I remember hearing a friend of mine telling his girl friend that if she gets pregnant that she will be on her own and that he will be emotionally unavailable for her. I remember thinking that was what I aspired to be like. Today, I can see that the only reason why things like that impressed me so much was that I didn't have the courage and tenacity to be myself. As I think about this and how people perceive me I understand that intimacy is a two part characteristic. First, I need to have the honesty to look inside myself and accept myself for the person I am regardless of my strengths and weaknesses. Second, I need to have the willingness to share that revelation with others and not to be overly concerned with how they will react or perceive me. This second part has always been a big problem for me. Even as a young child and having been given an example of what a truly loving relationship consist of and what must be done to maintain that relationship intimacy was never a big part of the equation. As much as I knew that my parents loved each other the word love was never a big part of their communication with each other.

I remember seeing couples walking down the street holding hands and sharing their intimate feeling for one another in public and not caring what others might think of it. I would look upon them as squares and non-hip individuals. Today, I can honestly say that I was jealous and envious of them because I never had the internal strength to do what they were doing because I was always concerned about if some of my peer group saw me that they would tease me. I was fearful that they would make certain comments to me like "she really has your nose wide open" or "now I know who wears the pants in that relationship" or the worst one "your brother would never be seen doing that." I remember when I was in England and went on vacation to Paris, France I had the opportunity to see real true intimacy in action. People were displaying their true affections for one anther and were not concerned or ashamed about what people might think about it. It didn't matter if it was men with other men or women with other women or men with women and vice versa the affection they had for one another was stronger than any perception of what other people might think about it. For the first time I was getting a little glimpse of what true intimacy consist of. I remember hearing a motivational speaker talk about true intimacy and he was talking about coming from an environment where men never show their true feelings to their mate or show any signs of vulnerability. Then after discussing this he posed a question to the audience. "How do you tell your mate that you are sexually intimated by her?" How do you admit to yourself and others that the square individuals like one's father who only wanted to raise a family and do the right things for them and their community is the person today that you aspire to become and not caring what others reaction to that type of lifestyle might be.

To fully understand and appreciate the full value of the benefits of intimacy with one's self it is extremely important to understand and appreciate the process one had to go through to build up one's self esteem and self worth. This process would allow an individual the willingness to share one's true self with another human being once that person has been revealed to oneself.

To start to receive the benefits of intimacy I needed to take an honest look at myself and allow the answer to many of the questions that have been posed above to be evident in the way I live my life. If I want people to look and treat me differently than they have been then I need to give them a reason to. Therefore, I need to start treating myself differently and do things that are not necessarily a good thing to do for myself but the right thing to do. Like anything else in life this would be a process that would not be accomplished over night. It is something that would be achieved over a period of time. I fond myself needing to build up my self esteem and self worth and I started doing that by setting goals for myself and seeing them through. All my life I would say that I was going to do this or do that and never see anything through to the end. My first goal that I set for myself was to stop using drugs completely and learn to deal with life on life terms without the aid of any external entities. As of April 5, 1995 so far I have accomplished that goal. My second goal was to go back to school and gain myself a college education. I started my quest on that goal in January of 1997. As of today I have achieved my high school diploma, an Associates Degree in Human Services, a Bachelor's Degree in Political Science, and an presently two semesters away from receiving my Master's Degree in Public Administration. I do not know if that one will be accomplished due to the health problems that I am experiencing today which has made it virtually impossible for me to return to college. Due to the types of grades that I generated while at the university I was given the opportunity of studying for my last semester for my Bachelors Degree in London, England. I have received numerous certificates for being on the dean's list. I was even given the honor of being inducted into the Honor Society of the university that I was attending.

While in college I decided another goal that I wanted to achieve was to become actively involved in school politics. Like anything else in life I knew that this was something that had to be done in small increments a little at a time. It would be a methodological process that I would undertake step by step. So the first thing for me in school was to find a club that interested me and become a member of that club. Even though I was African American I joined the Orguello Latino Club at the junior college I was attending. My reason behind that was for once in my life to have some diversity in my life. I needed to make real friends regardless of their age, race, sex, or religion. For once in my life I was noticing that the more I was getting involved and thinking of others more than just myself the better I was starting to feel about myself. From there I went to becoming involved in student government. I went from being the representative for the Orguello Latino club to secretary of student government to vice president of student government to president of student government. I need to say that this process took me to the head of student government in less than a year. For the first time I was allowing others with more experience in doing the right thing to guide me. One of the biggest steps I took to develop this concept of intimacy was to become involve with what at this time was called a mentor program. This was a program designed especially for minority students to choose a faculty member or administrative member to act as their role model. My life really began to change for the better when I ask the president of the university to be my mentor. He basically gave me card blanche to see him whenever I had things I needed to talk about regardless of how busy and involved with other things he might be. He shared with me how he came from an environment where people thought and told him to his face that he would never amount to anything and would be a failure. That was the motivation he needed to prove them all wrong. He went from getting his Bachelors degree to getting his law degree. I remember he told me hold when studying for his Bachelor's degree he would paint houses on the side for the extra money so he could continue with his education. From getting his law degree he went to being a prosecutor in the area where he lived. From there he went to becoming president of various junior colleges one after another. The thing that really stood out for me was his success did not come overnight. It came by taking and tackling one goal at a time and with each goal being accomplished his feelings of self-esteem and self worth was increasing.

So I took my lead from President Israel. The important thing for me was that I set my ambitions one goal at a time. As I accomplished each goal I found myself feeling better about myself. As I was becoming involved in all of these extra school activities it was important for me to stay focused on the reason why I was there and that was to get an education and do the very best that I was capable of doing. For the first time in my life my academic progress was amazing. I always new I had the ability to succeed but I never applied myself. I found myself going from being an average student to an honor student. I found myself taking some of the most difficult courses offered there and not just passing but excelling in those courses. From there I took it to the next level by becoming more involved in student government on the campus level. The next thing I did was to become involved in local politics in my community. I recall going to the local Freeholders meetings and I would just sit there and listen because I wanted to get an understanding of how the local county money was being spent. I remember I would always hear about open space and the county spending large amount of money in purchasing open space. It wasn't until I started going to these meetings that I understood the concept behind why they were purchasing so many acres of open space. I joined the local Human Relations Council and became involved with working to bring unity and consolidation to the community.

My next step would be to take my political interest to the state level. I did that by taking on the presidency of a statewide student run organization which sole purpose was representing students statewide at the statehouse. In this position I made myself available to student governments statewide and became highly educated in the state judicial and legislative process.

The more I was becoming involved in this process and helping others the more I found myself feeling good about myself. I was beginning to feel worthwhile and not useless. I was beginning to feel a part of my society and not a detriment to my society. I found myself beginning to form true and meaningful relationships with people, which I still have till this very day. I found myself not needing to always be around people to feel good about myself because of the things that I was doing I was starting to begin to build an intimate relationship with others and myself. I found myself in the beginning stages of opening up to others and trusting that they would not see my vulnerabilities as weaknesses but as part of the total makeup of the person I am. The most important part of this intimacy process was that I was beginning to love myself and my loving myself I found myself being able to love others.

BENEFITS OF INTIMACY

So what are the benefits of intimacy and how can they help to improve the quality of my life? When I look at these benefits the first thing that comes to mind is the development of an honest relationship with myself. This relationship is based on the foundation of accepting myself as the person I actually am. I've arrived at the point in my life where I no longer have to adopt certain philosophies that I do not believe in so that others will accept me. I am now at a point in my life where I am in touched with the fact that if someone is not willing to accept me as I am then I really do not need them as a part in my life. Today, I am able to look at myself in the mirror and be satisfied and content with the person that is looking back at me. Today, I am able to set goals and ambitions that I want to achieve and know that the reasons behind those goals are for self-satisfaction and not that to impress others. Intimacy has allowed me today to achieve reflective and reasonable clarity on who I am today, who I want to be in the future and what I need to do to achieve these goals of the future. Another benefit of intimacy for myself is the ability to set reasonable limitations on things I want to achieve and believing within myself that I can accomplish them. Today I realize that the only limitations I have on my life is the limitations I put on myself. I remember when I was at this junior college one of the guidance counselors was being interviewed for an article that was being written about me. The one thing that she said that really impressed her with me was my tenacity. She had suggested that I take 12 credits to start out with but I had decided I was going to take 20 credits. Her main concern was that I had been out of school for over twenty years and thought I should take my time being incorporated back into the academic system. Because I was starting to have confidence in myself and my own abilities I had faith that I would be able to accomplish this and at the same time not just get passing grades but to excel in my classes, which I did.

Now, as I look and see how the development of intimacy within my own life has allowed me the opportunity to get to know myself and become acquainted with my limitations and assets I am now able to look and see how intimacy has affected my relationships with other people.

Now that I am beginning to see the formation of trust and honor and faith within my own self I am able to allow those qualities to form relationships with other people. I have never before had intimate relationships with other people, especially someone of the opposite sex, mainly due to my fear of rejection and humiliation. I have learned lately that either I go out in faith and trust and believe in other people or live my life isolated within my own shell. Today, I understand that is no way to live and more important it is a way I do not want to live anymore. So now that I am at these crossroads what do I do to reap the benefits of intimacy and get past the constant fear of what if. I realize that making a decision is pointless unless it is followed by some sort of action. So now that I have made this decision what is the action that must follow to achieve the benefits of intimacy.

The action I must take needs to be done with the knowledge and understanding that whatever I do I cannot predict the outcome of these situations. I need to realize that I can not determine what is going to succeed or what is going to fail, but I need to have the willingness of heart to try. I was told one time that nothing beats a failure than an unwillingness to try. I need to believe and internalize the concept that if one door closes another one will open. Just like I gave my all in my active addiction I must give my all in working towards relationships born out of intimacy. I also need to believe that the perception of what and how people will act or receive me is just a faulty illusion in my mind that has clouded my reasonable judgement of what people are really like. If it need be I must allow people to reject and have faith that I will not completely fall apart and that I will be able to knock the dust off and keep on walking.

These are the things I need to do to get past my fear of intimacy. I'll let you know how everything comes out in my next book, but until then remember "If I can get through this –you can to!!!"

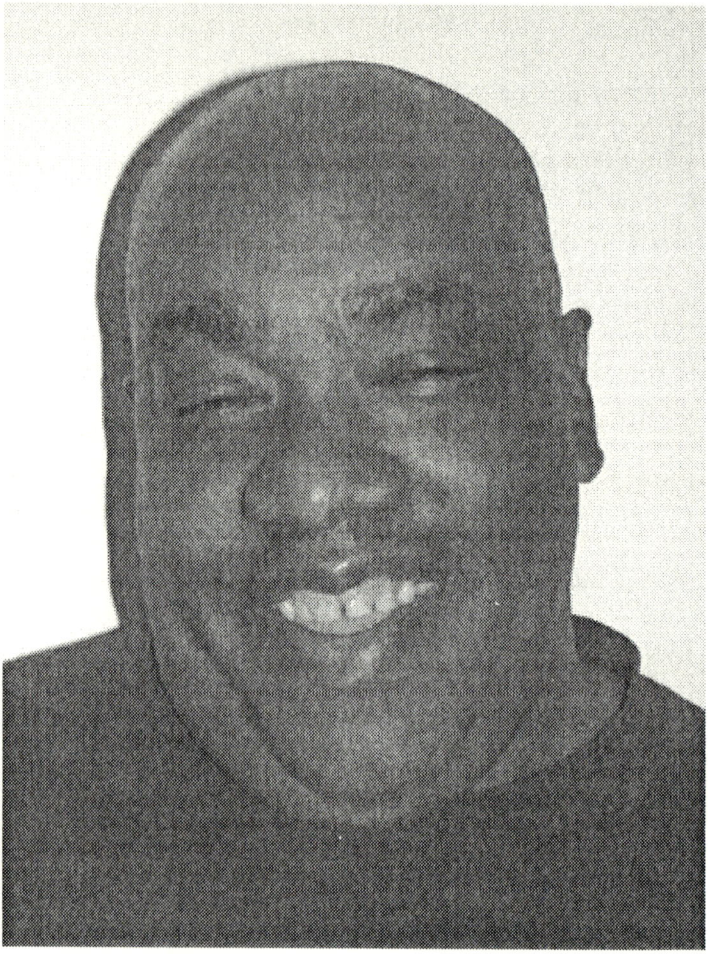

ABOUT THE AUTHOR

The author, Andre Gilchrist, is a middle aged African American who resides in the state of New Jersey. Through his involvement in the military and Viet Nam Conflict has been exposed to a wide variety of life's experiences and life's diversities.

The author comes from a middle class family which consisted of his mother, father and brother who are all deceased now. Through his life's trials and tribulations the author has had many highs and lows in his life.

Considering the barriers and obstacles in his life the author has had to overcome during his past life experiences, the author has made a miraculous recovery in improving his life and helping his fellow man. The author has garnished a number of awards and degrees which are a testament to his hard work and dedication to improving his life and the lives of all around him.

The author has been and continues to be a leader in his community, deeply involved in community activities, in both social and political commitments. His tenacity and enthusiasm bode well for his success in his present and future life. The author has demonstrated pure determination as well as a desire to learn and create positive changes in his life and his community.

The author credits Professor Tucker and Carroll Wilson, of Raritan Valley Community College English Department, for cultivating and improving his love of the English word into a form of communication that is easily understood by all who reads or hears his thoughts and words.

The author has risen to local and statewide prominence as an advocate and spokesperson for the less fortunate, especially in the area of higher education. The author has appeared on television, has been interviewed by local and state reporters and continues to live his life in a way to let all those around him know that "If he can change then they can to."

Printed in the United States
48245LVS00003B/287